COLLINS

Best
PLANTS

A N N E   S W I T H I N B A N K

HarperCollins*Publishers*
London

HarperCollins*Publishers*
London

❖

First published in 1999 by HarperCollins*Publishers*

Design and layout © HarperCollins*Publishers* 1999
Text: © Anne Swithinbank 1999

A catalogue record for this book is available
from the British Library.

ISBN 0-00-414105-9

Designed and produced for HarperCollins*Publishers* by
Cooling Brown, Middlesex, England
Editorial: Carole McGlynn, Ann Kay
Design: Alistair Plumb, Tish Mills
Photography: Peter Anderson, Steve Gorton

For HarperCollins*Publishers*
Editorial Director: Polly Powell
Managing Editor: Becky Humphries
Production Manager: David Lennox

Colour origination: Colourscan

Printed and bound in Great Britain by Scotprint

Contents

❖

INTRODUCTION

❖

4

WITH THOUSANDS OF CULTIVATED PLANTS to choose from, selecting those to suit us and our gardens presents a real challenge. Not only are there many different kinds of plant, but even within one type, for instance roses or clematis, there are hundreds if not thousands of cultivars. This can make a trip to the garden centre or the perusal of a nursery catalogue almost bewildering. In this book I suggest different sites and situations for which I recommend some of my favourite plants. Most of these I have grown myself at one time or another, and the remainder I would love to have the opportunity to try.

A lot of plants are chosen by impulse and while this is an exciting way to buy plants, it doesn't always result in the best planned garden. By using this book, you will at least become more focused in your shopping forays. Before rushing out, think hard about the role your next batch of plants are going to play in the garden. For example, some ground cover plants might keep weeds down, a bare fence could be crying out for a climber or two, or an injection of extra colour needed for late summer. Find the relevant section and take a look at the plant selection there, perhaps making a shortlist of your own.

During the development of this book, I have moved house, leaving behind my lovingly created garden of ten years. While wholly ready for the challenge of a new garden in a different part of the country, I already have a yearning to use my own book not only to replace some of my sorely missed

◁ **YOU WILL FIND** *many of the plants for sale at your local garden centre but less common ones are rewarding enough to order by post from specialist nurseries.*

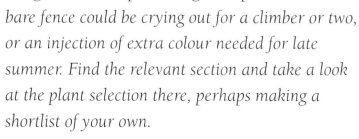

◁ **PROVIDED YOU CHOOSE PLANTS** *to suit their particular situation, with the right care you should be able to enjoy a colourful display each summer.*

favourite plants, but to take advantage of a different site and climate to try others. I'm bound to make a few substitutions and I can guarantee one or two impulse buys – and so must you, for the sake of individuality. But I shall avoid buying plants I don't have room for, since they sit and mope reproachfully in their pots, needing watering, feeding and planting.

In many ways, the researching and writing of this book has been an indulgence, like writing the ultimate plant shopping list. At the same time I have taken very seriously the responsibility for deciding which plants to include and which to leave out.

Each plant description is accompanied by symbols, some of which refer to the plant's hardiness. Those awarded three stars (❋❋❋) should be fully hardy and able to tolerate temperatures down to -15°C(5°F). Those with two stars (❋❋) could be described as frost hardy and will withstand temperatures down to about -5°C(23°F). One star (❋) indicates only half-hardiness, with plants rarely surviving temperatures below 0°C (32°F). The few tender plants included have no star but are given a minimum temperature. The leaf symbols tell you whether a plant is evergreen or deciduous. Some plants sport a cup-shaped symbol next to their name (♀), indicating they have been awarded the Royal Horticultural Society's Award of Garden Merit. To achieve this, their display must represent good value in the garden, they should be easy to care for, readily available and not greatly prone to pests and diseases.

ANNE SWITHINBANK

Trees for small gardens

Where space is restricted it makes sense to choose a tree with as many attributes as possible. Expect them to pay double or triple rent for their space and offer, perhaps, spring blossom, colourful fruits and autumn colour or beautiful foliage and attractive bark. Trees like birches make very suitable contenders, despite their height, because they cast comparatively little shade.

Acer japonicum 'Aconitifolium'

6

Acer japonicum 'Aconitifolium' ♔
Aconite-leaved maple
☼ ☽ ❄ ❄ ❄ ○ **H/S** 3m/10ft

This delightful cultivar bears rounded yet deeply lobed leaves, toothed around the edges. Fresh lime green spring foliage accompanies clusters of small red flowers, pale seedpods appear in summer and its autumn tints are rich crimson. Give all Japanese maples a moist but well-drained soil in a sheltered position as they dislike waterlogging and exposure to wind.

Amelanchier lamarckii ♔
Snowy mespilus
☼ ☽ ❄ ❄ ❄ ○ **H/S** 8m/25ft

Delicate white spring blossom contrasts prettily with silky, copper-tinged young leaves and is followed by black fruits.

The leaves turn orange-red in autumn. To encourage a tree-like shape, buy a standard-trained plant or select one or more main stems and prune out others. Plant in well-drained, lime-free soil.

Betula albosinensis var. *septentrionalis* ♔
Chinese red birch
☼ ☽ ❄ ❄ ❄ ○ **H** 18m/60ft **S** 6m/20ft

Although tall, most birches are slender and their dainty leaves cast little shade. In smaller gardens, those with beautiful trunks will give year-round pleasure. This choice Chinese birch bears a rich orange-pink peeling bark, pale and satiny when newly exposed. It also has spring catkins and yellow autumn leaves.

Cornus controversa 'Variegata' ♔
Table dogwood
☼ ☽ ❄ ❄ ❄ ○ **H/S** 6m/20ft

Although slow-growing, the wait is worthwhile for this delightful small tree, grown for its foliage. Tiered branches bear narrow, pointed leaves with irregular creamy margins. Tiny white flowers appear in early summer in large, flat clusters, followed by blue-black fruit. Plant in humus-rich, neutral to acid soil and shelter from spring frosts.

Genista aetnensis ♔
Mount Etna broom
☼ ❄ ❄ ❄ ○ **H/S** 8m/25ft

Few flowering trees match the display of fragrant, pea-like yellow flowers that this tall broom makes in early summer. The weeping, almost leafless, bright green stems are attractive too. Choose a free-draining soil and sheltered site as wind rock will shorten a plant's life. It tolerates poor, drought-prone, stony soils.

Malus floribunda ♔
Japanese crab apple
☼ ☽ ❄ ❄ ❄ ○ **H/S** 10m/30ft

Surely the most stunning of crab apples when its fleeting display of red buds opens to pale pink blooms that smother the canopy. Small fruits make little impact. Choose *M. x robusta* 'Red Sentinel' ♔ for white blossom and red fruits which last well past midwinter.

Prunus serrula ♔
Tibetan cherry
☼ ❄ ❄ ❄ ○ **H/S** 6–10m/20–30ft

One of my favourite trees, this makes a fine lawn specimen when sited to catch winter sun. There is year-round beauty in the rich

Amelanchier lamarckii

Prunus serrula

Eucalyptus pauciflora subsp. *niphophila*

red-brown bark, constantly peeling away to reveal brighter patches beneath. A smattering of small white flowers in spring is followed by dainty, narrow leaves. Grow as a standard tree or buy a stooled specimen with several trunks.

Pyrus salicifolia 'Pendula' ♀
Weeping silver pear

☼ ✳ ✳ ✳ ✿ **H** 5m/15ft **S** 4m/12ft

Weeping branches sweep down to the ground, making a waterfall of long, narrow silvery leaves all summer. Use to fill a corner or as a backdrop to other plants in a wide border. Creamy-white

△ **MALUS FLORIBUNDA** *The spreading branches of this small tree are smothered by such a wealth of spring blossom that the emerging leaves almost disappear.*

flowers in early spring are a bonus. If specimens become too wide, prune some stems back to the top in winter.

Robinia pseudoacacia 'Frisia' ♀
Golden false acacia

☼ ✳ ✳ ✳ ✿ **H** 9m/30ft **S** 6m/20ft

This small to medium tree is widely used where its leaves, composed of many rounded leaflets, bring a welcome splash of golden-yellow. Provide shelter from strong winds, especially while young plants are establishing. To restrict height, weigh down the ends of young branches to create a slight weeping habit.

Salix caprea 'Kilmarnock' ♀
Kilmarnock willow

☼ ✳ ✳ ✳ ✿ **H** 2–3m/6–10ft **S** 2m/6ft

This miniature weeping willow offers a good winter outline of yellow-brown stems, studded by silvery catkins with yellow anthers in late winter. Oval, toothed leaves are grey-green beneath. Trees mature into a wide umbrella shape.

SMALL TREE SELECTION
❖

Acer griseum (paperbark maple) ♀ ✿

Betula utilis var. *jacquemontii* ♀ ✿

Cornus alternifolia 'Argentea'
(silver pagoda dogwood) ♀ ✿

Eucalyptus pauciflora subsp.
niphophila (snow gum) ♀ ●

Gleditsia triacanthos 'Sunburst'
(honey locust) ♀ ✿

Prunus x *subhirtella* 'Autumnalis'
(winter cherry) ♀ ✿

SUPPORTING TREES
❖

There are two basic approaches to tree staking; rely on common sense to judge which is best for your tree. For most sturdy young trees, drive a short stake into the ground at an angle (*see below*). For trees with weak trunks unable to stand upright on their own, a better method involves driving a taller stake into the ground, parallel to the tree, some 15cm (6in) away from the trunk, so it reaches the point at which the branches start. Attach the stem to the stake in one or two places, using tree ties.

For some specimens I prefer to create a support 45cm (18in) high by making a cross-piece out of two uprights, 30cm (12in) away from the trunk on each side, with a horizontal piece of wood between them. Tie the stem into the horizontal, using a flexible material that will not rub (like nylon tights). Guide stakes close to the stems of bare-rooted trees between roots in the planting hole, but avoid driving stakes through the rootball of containerized trees.

STAKING A TREE *Insert a short stake in the ground at a 45° angle, on the side of the tree from which the wind mostly blows. Using a tree tie, attach the stem to it, about 45cm (18in) above ground.*

KEY: ♀ *Award of Merit* ☼ *sun* ☀ *semi-shade* ● *shade* ✳ *half-hardy* ✳✳ *frost-hardy* ✳✳✳ *fully hardy* ✿ *deciduous* ● *evergreen* ✿ *semi-evergreen* **H** *height* **S** *spread*

Trees with fruit and berries

Planting trees that bear attractive fruits not only brings colour to the garden during autumn, but provides a valuable natural larder for birds in the colder weather. Make sure you position berrying trees where you can watch the birds from a house window.

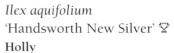

Mespilus germanica

Arbutus × *andrachnoides* ♔
Strawberry tree

☀ ✳ ✳ ✳ ◗ **H/S** 8m /25ft

This hybrid between *A. andrachne* and *A. unedo* is found naturally in Greece and offers much to a garden. Its attributes include peeling cinnamon bark, evergreen leaves and small, white, bell-shaped flowers that appear during spring or autumn. They usually coincide with the ripening of last season's rounded fruits as they turn through orange to red. Although strictly edible, the fruits are barely palatable. *Arbutus* tolerates chalk, but need a sheltered position away from cold winds.

Catalpa bignonioides ♔
Indian bean tree

☀ ✳ ✳ ✳ ◯ **H/S** 4.5–15m /25–50ft

The spreading canopy of this North American tree is impressive enough, due to the exotic appearance of the large, roughly heart-shaped leaves. The effect is compounded by panicles of flowers like chubby white foxgloves spotted with yellow and purple. These appear in summer, followed by a display of curious, bean-like pods to 38cm (15in) long. Plant in good, well-drained soil and avoid exposed positions.

Cotoneaster frigidus
Himalayan tree cotoneaster

☀ ◐ ✳ ✳ ✳ ◯◗ **H/S** 6m /20ft

Trees sold under this species name may be the true species or one of the hybrids more correctly described as *C.* × *watereri*. Either way, you can expect a robust, deciduous or semi-evergreen tree bearing long, oval leaves and flat clusters of small white flowers in early summer, followed by a splendid crop of bright red berries that last into winter.

Ilex aquifolium
'Handsworth New Silver' ♔
Holly

☀ ✳ ✳ ✳ ◗ **H** 8m /25ft **S** 4.5m /15ft

My favourite among the variegated hollies, this beauty eventually grows to a small, vaguely columnar tree. Prickly, mottled leaves have distinct, creamy-white margins and grow from attractive purple stems. Being a female form, bright red berries will be produced if there is a male holly in the vicinity.

Juglans regia ♔
Common walnut

☀ ✳ ✳ ✳ ◯ **H** 18m /60ft **S** 9m /30ft

Walnuts make beautiful trees which, with their long history of cultivation, lend great character to a garden. Their pinnate leaves are attractive and their edible nuts develop inside greenish fruits. Plant selected clones such as 'Buccaneer' for earlier, better crops of nuts. Current breeding programmes are in the process of creating improved trees. Avoid frost pockets when planting.

Ilex aquifolium 'Handsworth New Silver'

HOW TO CHOOSE?

- Some trees, like rowans (*Sorbus*) make a mess when their berries drop, or are thrown about by birds. Avoid siting these near paths and patios, which might become stained and slippery.

- Some fruits and berries, such as those of yew and ivy, are poisonous and a hazard to young children.

- Wildlife enthusiasts may wish to plant fruiting trees to supply birds with food in winter. Hawthorn (*Crataegus*), rowan (*Sorbus*) and red-berried hollies (*Ilex*) are best value.

- Those who make their own jams, jellies and wines will welcome fruiting trees as a source of natural ingredients: damsons, crab apples and medlar are good choices.

BEAT THE BIRDS

❖

In general, birds tend to go first for red and orange berries, leaving pink or white ones until last. So the fruits of *Malus* 'Golden Hornet', *Sorbus* 'Joseph Rock' and *S. cashmiriana* tend not to be the birds' first choice. But *Malus* 'Red Sentinel' stays untouched.

◁ SORBUS CASHMIRIANA *Sorbus like this pretty Kashmir rowan are easy to raise from seed. Simply squash the ripe berries, extract their seed and sow into pots. Cover lightly with grit and set them outdoors to germinate.*

Koelreuteria paniculata ♀
Golden rain tree, Pride of India

☼ ❋ ❋ ❋ ○ **H/S** 9m/30ft

The chief features of this excellent tree are its fine, pinnate foliage and the panicles of yellow flowers produced in summer, followed later by the pink-flushed, bladder-like fruit capsules. Yellow leaf tints provide its finale for the year. This Chinese native can be tricky to establish, but thrives on a fertile, loamy soil and, given plenty of sun, it will flower and fruit even when young.

Malus 'John Downie' ♀
Crab apple

☼ ❋ ❋ ❋ ○ **H** 7.5m/25ft **S** 5m/16ft

Clusters of the luminous orange and red fruits of this tree appearing against a blue, late-summer sky is one of my favourite sights as the season draws to a close. These oval crab apples are edible and can be used to make jelly. There is also a good display of white blossom, opening from pink buds during late spring. The crab apple thrives in any fertile, well-drained soil.

Mespilus germanica
Medlar

☼ ☼ ❋ ❋ ❋ ○ **H** 6m/20ft **S** 8m/26ft

This tree of great character blooms in early summer, producing a sprinkling of large, solitary white flowers. These are followed by distinctive brown fruits

Malus 'John Downie'

that make a good jelly but can be eaten raw only when left until half-rotten. Trees generally take on a low, gnarled shape and often bear spines on their mature branches.

Prunus insititia 'Prune Damson'
Damson

☼ ❋ ❋ ❋ ○ **H/S** 3–6m/10–20ft

White spring blossom and good crops of oval, blue-black fruits are features of this damson. The greeny yellow-fleshed fruits are superb in tarts and jams. Damsons are robust and grow well on most soils, including poor ones.

Sorbus cashmiriana ♀
Kashmir rowan

☼ ☼ ❋ ❋ ❋ ○ **H/S** 6m/20ft

In contrast to its size and daintiness, this tree bears comparatively large heads of pink-flushed flowers in late spring. By autumn, these have developed into beautiful white fruits. Birds are not fond of these, so they are usually left, hanging by red stalks, long after the leaves have fallen. Plant in moist, well-drained soil.

Flowering and fruiting hedges

The leafy backdrop created by a good hedge makes a pleasing boundary. Hedges also play a role as living screens and dividers within gardens, with their good looks and natural appearance. As well as acting as barriers, hedges filter noise and wind and can be used to obscure unsightly views. To match the style of a garden, choose plants carefully, taking into account their size and whether a formal or informal hedge will suit the design. Heights and spreads are given for the plants when grown (and clipped) as a hedge.

10

Berberis × stenophylla ♛
Barberry

☼ ☀ ✳ ✳ ✳ ✿

H 1.2–1.8m /4–6ft **S** 75–90cm /2ft 6in–3ft

This evergreen hybrid makes a dense, spiny, virtually impenetrable hedge of generally formal appearance. Arching shoots bear golden-yellow flowers in spring, followed by purple berries that are often removed by trimming. Plant in autumn or early spring, 50cm (20in) apart, immediately pruning off the top quarter of growth to promote bushiness. Trim annually after flowering.

Cotoneaster simonsii ♛
☼ ✳ ✳ ✳ ✿ **H** 1.2–1.5m /4–5ft **S** 90cm /3ft

Choose this cotoneaster for an informal, semi-evergreen hedge decorated with bright orange-red berries as the leaves turn red in autumn. There is a display of pink-tinged, white flowers in early summer. Plant from autumn to spring, setting them 35cm (14in) apart. If possible, use secateurs to prune back long stems after flowering, leaving developing berry clusters. Tidy up again during late summer and autumn.

Escallonia 'Apple Blossom' ♛
☼ ✳ ✳ ✳ ✿ **H** 1.5m /5ft **S** 90cm /3ft

Although escallonias are slightly tender, they make good, dense hedges of quite formal appearance in sheltered areas. Being salt-tolerant, they thrive near mild coastlines. The glossy, evergreen leaves of this variety are joined by pale pink flowers during summer. E. 'Langleyensis' ♛ is hardier and a good dark pink. Plant in spring or autumn, 45cm (18in) apart. Trim the top third back after planting to encourage bushiness. Prune lightly after flowering.

Forsythia × intermedia 'Lynwood' ♛
☼ ✳ ✳ ✳ ✪ **H** 2.5m /8ft **S** 90cm–1.2m /3–4ft

Forsythias form rather gangly, informal hedges but they certainly make their presence felt in spring when smothered with bright yellow flowers. Their ability to thrive almost everywhere has ensured them great popularity. Plant in the autumn at 45cm (18in) intervals, pruning by one third to promote growth. Remove older stems after flowering.

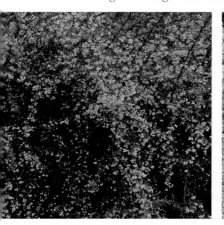

Garrya elliptica
Silk tassel bush
☼ ☀ ✳ ✳ ✿

H 1.5–2.2m /5–7ft **S** 90cm /3ft

Choose this evergreen for a stylish informal hedge. Set against a backdrop of leathery, grey-green leaves from winter to spring is a display of beautiful, pale green catkins. Males (the showiest) and females are

Berberis × stenophylla   *Forsythia × intermedia 'Lynwood'*   *Garrya elliptica*

◁ ROSA RUGOSA
*The hedgehog rose
should not be dead-
headed as this would
rob the garden of its
plump hips which are
such a welcome feature
in late summer and
into autumn.*

11

borne on separate plants, so it pays to select a male clone like 'James Roof' ♉, whose silvery catkins are 20cm (8in) long. Plant 45cm (18in) apart in autumn or spring and prune hedges back with secateurs after the tassels have faded.

Osmanthus x burkwoodii ♉
☼ ☼ ✳ ✳ ✳ ❦

H 1.5–1.8m /5–6ft **S** 75–90cm /2ft 6in–3ft

A neat but informal hedge of glossy, dark green leaves sprinkled liberally with clusters of small, white, sweetly scented flowers in spring. Plant 45cm (18in) apart during winter, trimming any spreading plants back by up to one third in spring to encourage a bushy shape. Tackle regular pruning after flowering in late spring.

Pyracantha 'Watereri' ♉
Firethorn
☼ ☼ ✳ ✳ ✳ ❦

H 2–2.5m /6–8ft **S** 75–90cm /2ft 6in–3ft

This glossy-leaved shrub will make a good informal hedge; it bears clusters of small white flowers in spring and

bright red berries during late summer and autumn. Tough and reliable, it grows well on most soils but can be susceptible to fireblight. Plant 60cm (2ft) apart between autumn and spring. Prune carefully after flowering, leaving the developing berries to ripen.

Ribes sanguineum
'Pulborough Scarlet' ♉
Flowering currant
☼ ✳ ✳ ✳ ♡ **H** 1.5–1.8m /5–6ft **S** 90cm–1.2m /3–4ft

Despite their somewhat acrid smell, flowering currants make splendid informal floriferous hedges in spring. This cultivar bears racemes of red flowers, but there are those with white (*R.s.*'Tydeman's White' ♉), pink and pale pink blooms. Set young plants 45cm (18in) apart from autumn to spring and prune back directly after flowering.

Rosa rugosa
Hedgehog rose
☼ ✳ ✳ ✳ ♡ **H** 1.5m /5ft **S** 1.2m /4ft

Choose this rose to make a delightful informal hedge for the boundary of a large garden. Its growth may be a little

unruly, but the fragrant, single, pinkish-red roses, followed by a display of bold hips, more than compensate for it. Look for white-flowered *R.r.* 'Alba' ♉ and strongly scented, purple-red, double-flowered *R.* 'Roseraie de l'Häy' ♉. Plant 45cm (18in) apart from autumn to spring and prune in early spring by removing weak and unwanted growth.

Rosmarinus officinalis
Rosemary
☼ ✳ ✳ ✳ ❦

H 1.3–1.5m /4–5ft **S** 75–90cm /2ft 6in–3ft

Rosemary makes a fragrant and beautiful informal hedge, and will even produce some flowers during mild spells in winter. The flowers vary from purple-blue to white and contrast well with the needle-like, grey-green leaves. The habit of this shrub is naturally upright, but to accentuate this, choose *R.o.* 'Miss Jessopp's Upright' ♉. Plant 38cm (15in) apart in spring or autumn and prune during midsummer.

THORNY BOUNDARIES
❖

Some gardens need a tough, impenetrable, thorny barrier. Hedges have a lot to offer here, as many hedging plants are armed with spines or thorns. There are instances where a fence or wall might seem tame by comparison with a hedge of berberis, holly, rose, hawthorn or even *Poncirus trifoliata*. The latter is the Japanese bitter orange often used as a stock for cultivated orange and lemon varieties; it will make a deciduous hedge, around 1.5m (5ft) tall, of rigid green shoots armed with vicious spines; fragrant white flowers are followed by small, inedible, orange-like fruit.

Evergreen shrubs for year-round interest

We use our gardens less during winter yet we still need to preserve an interesting outlook. To do this effectively, half to two-thirds of your shrubs should be evergreen. Include shrubs with a variety of different leaf colours and textures as well as good flowering shrubs and the effect will never be gloomy.

Drimys lanceolata

Aucuba japonica
Himalayan laurel, Spotted laurel

☼ ☼ ❄ ❄ ❄ ❄ ✿ **H/S** 1.8–2.5m/6–8ft

The best spotted form of the tough aucubas is *A.j.* 'Crotonifolia' ♔, a female form liberally speckled with yellow on bright green. However, to brighten a gloomy corner, opt for *A.j.* 'Picturata', a male whose leaves boast a central splash of gold. Though it has a tendency to revert, it does not take much effort to cut away green shoots as they appear.

Choisya ternata Sundance ♔
Golden Mexican orange blossom

☼ ☼ ❄ ❄ ❄ ✿

H 1.5m/5ft **S** 1.2–1.5m/4–5ft

This popular shrub deserves inclusion for its marvellous shining yellow foliage,

guaranteed to draw the eye. Despite this, I still prefer the plain-leaved *Choisya ternata*, for the contrast between its rich green leaves and its white, scented blossom in spring and late summer. Flowers are scarce on the golden form. Both will thrive in alkaline soil.

Cupressus macrocarpa 'Golden Pillar'
Golden Monterey cypress

☼ ❄ ❄ ❄ ❄ ✿ **H** 3–4.5m/10–15ft **S** 1.8–3m/6–10ft

I usually avoid the Monterey cypress on account of its thug-like tendency to grow fast and tall, but this cultivar is different. Its bright, golden-yellow foliage is stunning all year round and becomes a great asset to any border. It looks good planted next to green-, blue- and grey-leaved plants.

Acuba japonica 'Picturata'

VARIEGATED YEAR-ROUND EVERGREENS

❖

Elaeagnus × ebbingei 'Gilt Edge' ♔
Euonymus japonicus
'Ovatus Aureus' ♔
Ilex aquifolium 'Ferox Argentea' (holly)♔
Myrtus communis 'Variegata' (myrtle)
Pittosporum tenuifolium
'Irene Paterson' ♔

Drimys lanceolata
Mountain pepper

☼ ❄ ❄ ✿ **H** 2.5m/8ft **S** 1.8m/6ft

One of my favourite evergreens, this shrub seems to perform better in a cool, sheltered, lightly shaded spot than in full light. My plant has made a compact, loosely conical shape, 1.5m (5ft) tall, over a period of seven years. Dark red stems bear slender, sweetly aromatic, bright green young foliage and darker old leaves with pale undersides. They are joined by clusters of creamy-white flowers in late spring. Mulch with well-rotted leafmould in late winter. Hardy to -12°C (10°F).

Elaeagnus pungens 'Maculata' ♔
☼ ☼ ❄ ❄ ❄ ✿ **H/S** 2.5–3.7m/8–12ft

The winter garden would not be complete without a specimen of this tried and tested evergreen. Its leaves are gilded by an irregular central splash of golden yellow, leaving two tones of green around the outside. The undersides are pale and silvery, while the stems and midribs are metallic bronze-gold. Snip out any plain green shoots as and when they occur. Elaeagnus is a particularly useful shrub for seaside gardens as it will tolerate coastal winds.

12

◁ **CUPRESSUS MACROCARPA**
'GOLDEN PILLAR' has been enlivened
for summer by training a climbing
Ipomoea lobata through it.

that spray out attractively. Cut
out older stems of large shrubs
after flowering.

Nandina domestica ♀
Heavenly bamboo
☼ ☼ ✳ ✳ ✳ ✳ ●

H 1.2–1.8m / 4–6ft **S** 90–150cm / 3–5ft
The elegant shape and foliage
of this neat, bamboo-like shrub
are joined by panicles of white
flowers in midsummer. Young
leaves are a glowing red and the
older foliage takes on a bright
reddish-purple hue in winter. Red
fruits form, which turn black: for
the best fruit, choose *N.d.*
'Richmond'. This shrub needs
shelter from cold winds and a well-
drained soil to preserve its hardiness.

Photinia × *fraseri* 'Red Robin' ♀
☼ ☼ ✳ ✳ ● **H/S** 3–4.5m / 10–15ft
Choose this handsome shrub for its
pliable stems of long, leathery leaves,
which start off a brilliant bronze-red
when young. It makes a good alternative
to pieris where the soil is not acid

> ## SMALL OR LARGE?
> ❖
> Whether you are planting the entire
> garden from scratch or trying to
> establish the shrubby backbone of a
> border, it is tempting to buy time by
> buying big. One disadvantage is that
> prices rise in direct proportion to the
> length of time it took the nursery to
> grow the plant on. And shrubs that
> have become used to container-
> growing usually establish less well
> than smaller plants whose young roots
> develop more naturally in open soil.
> Buying young is more economical too.

enough. Suits most soils, but site well
away from frost pockets as new shoots
can be damaged by late frosts. Responds
well to pruning if size needs restricting.

Rhamnus alaternus
'Argenteovariegata' ♀
Variegated Italian buckthorn
☼ ☼ ✳ ✳ ✳ ✳ ●

H 1.8–4.5m / 6–15ft **S** 1.8–3m / 6–10ft
Some evergreens can be overbearing but
the small, silvery leaves of this rhamnus
ensure a delicate effect to brighten up
sheltered corners. Dark stems of grey-
green leaves have silvery-white margins
and can be trained up sunny walls or
clipped into rounded shapes.

13

Lonicera nitida 'Baggesen's Gold' ♀
☼ ☼ ✳ ✳ ✳ ✳ ● **H/S** 1.5m / 5ft
This common shrub provides a
welcome splash of gold all year and is
easy to grow in most gardens. Long
shoots bearing neat, oval leaves arch over
each other like a golden waterfall. The
small leaves create a texture that is
usefully juxtaposed against large-leaved
shrubs; the foliage can become bleached
in full sun. May be grown as a low hedge.

Mahonia × *media* 'Charity' ♀
☼ ☼ ✳ ✳ ✳ ✳ ● **H/S** 2.2–3.7m / 7–12ft
Any tall, evergreen, architectural shrub
that flowers in winter is worth its weight
in gold. The leaves of mahonia are about
60cm (2ft) long, comprising many dark
green, spiny leaflets. From late autumn
to late winter it bears erect racemes of
slightly scented, deep yellow flowers

Photinia × fraseri 'Red Robin'

Rhamnus alaternus 'Argenteovariegata'

Shrubs for spring colour

Spring is such an eagerly awaited season that it makes sense to plant for an early show, to create as long and as lively a season of colour and perfume as possible. Place shrubs for spring interest at intervals around your garden, underplanted with groups of bulbs and spring-flowering herbaceous perennials.

14

Berberis × lologensis 'Apricot Queen'

Berberis × lologensis 'Apricot Queen' ♛

☼ ☼ ❋ ❋ ❋ ❧ **H/S** 2.5–3m/8–10ft

In late spring, the arching stems of this colourful shrub are packed with beautiful, clear apricot-orange flowers; it often produces a secondary flush of bloom in summer. The small, dark, glossy leaves are armed with spines, making it an ideal deterrent. Prune, if necessary, after flowering.

Ceanothus 'Puget Blue' ♛
Californian lilac

☼ ❋ ❋ ❋ ❧ **H/S** 2.5–3m/8–10ft

The small, dark green leaves alone make this an attractive plant. By late spring and early summer, when it is smothered with masses of small, deep blue flowers, it becomes spectacular. Plant in the shelter of a warm wall or fence to give protection from the worst of the winter weather. Suits most soils; trim after flowering if needed.

Euphorbia characias ♛

☼ ❋ ❋ ❋ ❧ **H** 1.2m/4ft **S** 90–120cm/3–4ft

Stems resembling dense tails and furnished with long leaves are decorated from early spring to early summer by cylindrical heads of lime-green 'flowers', consisting mainly of bracts. I like the dark centres of the species, although the acid-yellow colouring of *E.c.* ssp. *wulfenii* ♛ is exceptionally fine. After flowering, it pays to cut the spent flower stems to within 15cm (6in) of the ground. This retains vigour and keeps the foliage fresh. Bear in mind that the milky sap of this plant can cause skin irritation.

× *Ledodendron* 'Arctic Tern' ♛

☼ ❋ ❋ ❋ ❧ **H/S** 60cm/24in

Take a close look at this cross between a rhododendron and a ledum, to appreciate its sinuous branches covered with smooth, pale brown bark. Neat foliage is present year-round, but the

Ceanothus 'Puget Blue'

small shrub comes alive with a mass of pure white blooms in spring. Provide an acid, humus-rich soil and find time to dead-head after flowering.

Magnolia stellata 'Waterlily' ♛
Star magnolia

☼ ❋ ❋ ❋ ❧ ◯ **H** 2.5m/8ft **S** 3m/10ft

Opening before the foliage, the white flowers of this cultivar are up to 13cm (5in) wide and packed with as many as 32 petals. Guaranteed to turn heads, this shrub will form the main attraction of a spring border. Young plants begin bushy but expand with age, so make provision for this when planting. Tolerates most soils, including alkaline, but appreciates moisture and organic matter.

Rhododendron luteum ♛
Common yellow azalea

☼ ❋ ❋ ❋ ❧ ◯ **H/S** 2–3m/6–10ft

Choose this azalea for its cheerful, sweetly perfumed yellow flowers, which herald warm weather by blooming in late spring and early summer. There is another display in autumn when the leaves turn crimson, purple and orange before falling. With its informal habit, this shrub lends itself to a wilder corner of the garden, where it could perhaps be underplanted with bluebells. It must have an acid soil.

> ## SCENTED SPRING-FLOWERING SHRUBS
> ❖
>
> *Corylopsis pauciflora* ♥ ○
> *Cytisus* × *praecox* 'Warminster' ♥ ○
> *Daphne* × *burkwoodii* 'Somerset' ●
> *Daphne laureola* ●
> *Erica arborea* var. *alpina* ♥ ●
> *Fothergilla gardenii* ○
> *Magnolia liliiflora* 'Nigra' ♥ ○
> *Osmanthus* × *burkwoodii* ♥ ●
> *Rhododendron mucronatum* ●

△ **BOLD CLUMPS OF** Euphorbia characias *subsp.* wulfenii *'John Tomlinson' bear acid-yellow flowerheads that show up well against the darker foliage.*

Rhododendron yunnanense

☼ ◑ ✳ ✳ ✳ ● ○ **H** 4.5m/15ft **S** 3m/10ft

Although this delightful rhododendron is hardly compact, I would choose it if my soil were acid enough. I have seen its variable white, pale pink or dark pink flowers with pretty, spotted throats laugh at late frosts that have devastated every other rhododendron in the same garden. Select a plant in bloom to be sure of picking a specific colour and plan a pretty, wild corner around it. Like most of its tribe, it prefers an area of cool atmosphere and high rainfall and must have an acid soil.

Stachyurus praecox ♥

☼ ◑ ✳ ✳ ✳ ○ **H/S** 1.5–2.5m/5–8ft

This Japanese native makes a strong feature in late winter and early spring, when its reddish-brown branches are strung with hanging racemes of small, greenish-yellow, bell-shaped flowers, like exotic catkins. These form during autumn and wait all winter on the plant. Prefers an acid, humus-rich soil, yet tolerates lime in the soil; dig in plenty of leafmould or well-rotted compost before planting.

Syringa vulgaris 'Congo'
Lilac

☼ ✳ ✳ ✳ ○ **H** 4.5m/15ft **S** 4m/12ft

Wandering around a late spring garden during dusk would not be the same without the scent of lilac. There are many cultivars with single and double flowers, in light or dark colours, from which to choose. This form dates from 1896 and makes a compact plant with deep purple buds opening to large heads of single, intensely lilac-purple flowers. Restrict the size by shortening older stems after flowering.

Viburnum carlesii 'Diana'

☼ ◑ ✳ ✳ ✳ ○ **H/S** 1.8m/6ft

With fresh, newly opened spring foliage as a foil, the pink flowerheads open from red buds, then fade to white. The sweet fragrance lingers in the air and is guaranteed to turn heads. The leaves, bronze-tinged when young, spend the summer as a green backdrop for other plants, then can show some reddish tints during autumn.

Magnolia liliiflora 'Nigra'

Rhododendron cv.

Stachyurus praecox

Shrubs for summer colour

With good planning, there can be a succession of colourful and interesting flowering shrubs performing from early summer to autumn. Once established, they are largely able to look after themselves, though most will benefit from an annual pruning. This improves flower quality, helps to control shape and size and can prolong the lives of otherwise short-lived shrubs.

Phygelius capensis

Buddleja × weyeriana
☼ ✽✽✽✽ ♡ **H** 1.8–3.7m /6–12ft **S** 1.5–3m /5–10ft

Buddlejas are reliable summer flowerers and this one can be guaranteed to light up a fading border. Both the arching shoots and new leaves are felted with greyish hairs when young. The honey-scented yellow flowers are held in clusters towards the ends of shoots. *B.×. 'Sungold'* ♥ bears bright golden-yellow flowers. Control the plant's height by pruning hard every spring.

PRUNING BUDDLEJA
❖

Buddlejas like *B. × weyeriana* and *B. davidii* are usually cut back hard in early spring as the buds swell. Leave them taller for the backs of borders. An autumn pruning is an option in milder areas.

Deutzia × rosea
☼ ✽✽✽✽ ♡ **H/S** 1.2m /4ft

This rounded, compact shrub flowers beautifully in early summer, when the arching branches become covered with soft pink, star-shaped flowers that blend well with stronger pinks and purples. It is best placed towards the front of a shrub border. Prune immediately after flowering by cutting up to one fifth of the oldest branches down to ground level and cut flowered shoots back to lower buds.

Fabiana imbricata f. violacea ♥
☼ ✽✽✽ ♥ **H/S** 1.5–2.2m /5–7ft

Although this unusual shrub resembles a giant heather, it belongs to the same family as potatoes, tomatoes and petunias. Its scale-like foliage is joined by a profusion of pale mauve, tubular

---

GOOD-VALUE SUMMER COLOUR
❖

Ceanothus × delileanus 'Gloire de Versailles' ♥ ♡
Cistus × hybridus ♥ ♥
Perovskia 'Blue Spire' ♥ ♡
Potentilla fruticosa 'Elizabeth' ♥ ♡
Weigela florida 'Foliis Purpureis' ♥ ♡

---

flowers from early to midsummer. Provide shelter from wind and a well-drained soil. Leggy plants can be pruned back in spring, but cutting into old wood can be a gamble.

Fuchsia magellanica 'Versicolor' ♥
☼ ☼ ✽✽✽ ♥ **H/S** 90cm–1.2m /3–4ft

Hardy fuchsias are easy to grow and bring useful colour to gardens during late summer. The superb foliage of this plant begins grey-green and white (or yellow), liberally flushed with purple-pink, and matures to a slatey green, irregularly edged with creamy white. The slim, tubular flowers are red and purple. Prune back frost-damaged stems in spring and remove any straggly branches. Will grow much larger in milder and coastal areas.

Hibiscus syriacus 'Red Heart' ♥
☼ ✽✽✽✽ ♡ **H** 1.8–3m /6–10ft **S** 1.2–1.8m /4–6ft

Although slow-growing, a mature, hardy hibiscus in full bloom is a wonderful sight. Hibiscus are among the last shrubs to burst into growth in spring and they wait until late summer before producing their large, trumpet-shaped blooms. This cultivar bears dramatic white flowers, 6cm (2½in) across, with dark maroon centres. Good for chalky soils. Pruning is not usually needed.

△ **FOR LASTING COLOUR** *choose shrubby mallows such as* Lavatera *'Rosea', which produces masses of flowers all summer long. It is seen here in a border with lavender and* Alchemilla mollis.

For best results, provide well-drained soil and shelter from cold winds. An annual hard pruning in early spring, to remove old growth, will rejuvenate a plant and help it to live longer.

Philadelphus 'Virginal' ♡
Mock orange

☼ ☼ ❋ ❋ ❋ ◯

H 2.5–3.7m /8–12ft **S** 1.8–2.5m /6–8ft

The deliciously sweet perfume of mock orange fills the early to midsummer air with fragrance. This form is vigorous and upright, bearing double flowers of purest white. Prune after flowering by removing a fifth of the oldest growths down to ground level. Cut flowered stems back to new, strong shoots lower down the stems.

Phygelius x *rectus*
'Winchester Fanfare'
Cape figwort

☼ ❋ ❋ ❋ ◐ **H/S** 75cm–1.2m /30in–4ft

In common with other Cape figworts, this cultivar provides great summer colour and, given a well-drained soil, is easy to grow. The tubular flowers, an unusual shade of orange-pink, hang from the stems like inverted trumpets. The foliage will die back during severe winters, but re-grows in spring.

Hydrangea serrata 'Bluebird' ♡
Blue lacecap hydrangea

☼ ☼ ❋ ❋ ❋ ◯ **H/S** 1.2m /4ft

Hydrangeas provide welcome late-summer colour and perform best when given a cool, moist root run and light shade. In classic lacecap fashion, a dome of blue fertile flowers forms a hazy centre surrounded by an abstract pattern of ray florets, which will vary in colour according to soil. On chalk, expect a reddish-purple tinge, while on acid soils they will be violet-blue. Prune by thinning or cutting back hard in spring.

Kolkwitzia amabilis
Beauty bush

☼ ❋ ❋ ❋ ◯

H 1.8–3m /6–10ft **S** 1.8–2.5m /6–8ft

Deep pink, tubular flowers with patterned, yellow throats smother the arching branches of this delightful shrub in early summer; look out for *K.a.* 'Pink Cloud' ♡, for its deep pink blooms. For the rest of the year it creates a leafy background. Easy to

please, the beauty bush tolerates a wide range of soils. Prune after flowering by shortening or removing up to a third of the flowered stems.

Lavatera 'Rosea' ♡
Tree mallow

☼ ❋ ❋ ❋ ◐ **H/S** 1.5–1.8m /5–6ft

For sheer long-standing, mid- to late summer flower power, this shrub is unbeatable; it is also easy to grow. Deep rosy-pink flowers 10cm (4in) across open profusely over grey-green leaves.

Hibiscus syriacus 'Red Heart'

Hydrangea serrata 'Bluebird'

Kolkwitzia amabilis

17

Shrubs for autumn colour

Autumn is a precious season, when the lowering rays of the sun seem especially designed to illuminate glorious autumn tints and voluptuous fruits. I like to savour the last warm days before the onset of winter and always plan for some seasonal surprises. Many shrubs perform during autumn as well as scoring high with spring or summer flowers.

Clerodendrum trichotomum

18

Calluna vulgaris 'Spook'
Ling, Scots heather

☼ ❈ ❈ ❈ ☙ **H** 45cm/18in **S** 45–60cm/18–24in

With its downy grey foliage, this ling has an ethereal quality enhanced by tall spikes of mauve flowers borne from late summer to early winter. The faded flowers remain of great value throughout winter, adding to its ghostly appearance, especially when shimmering with hoar frost. Shear off the dead flower stems in spring. Must have an acid soil.

Clerodendrum trichotomum var. fargesii ♔
☼ ❈ ❈ ❈ ♡ **H/S** 3.7–6m/12–20ft

This is one of my favourite shrubs. After a slow start in spring, large, dark green leaves make a bold show. Sprays of scented, starry white flowers appear from pink-flushed sepals during late summer and autumn, developing into jewel-like, turquoise berries sitting on calyces that resemble shocking pink cushions. Plant in a sheltered spot. Pruning is not usually required.

Calluna vulgaris 'Spook'

Cotinus 'Flame' ♔
Smoke bush

☼ ☼ ❈ ❈ ❈ ♡

H 3.7–6m/12–20ft **S** 3–4.5m/10–15ft

The delights of this large shrub include the summer display of long, pink-tinged flower plumes, which seem to hover above the foliage like smoke. There are pyrotechnics from the foliage in autumn, as it turns from light green to brilliant red and orange. Plant in moist, well-drained soil which, for the best tints, should not be too fertile. Prune out unwanted branches after flowering.

Euonymus alatus ♔
Winged spindle

☼ ☼ ❈ ❈ ❈ ♡ **H/S** 1.8–2.5m/6–8ft

This medium-sized shrub produces reliable autumn colour, even on alkaline soils, when the dark green leaves turn crimson-pink. Insignificant late spring flowers develop into round, reddish-purple fruit, some opening to reveal orange seeds. The leaves and fruits eventually fall to reveal stems with four cork-like wings running their length.

Fothergilla major ♔
☼ ☼ ❈ ❈ ❈ ♡

H 1.8–2.5m/6–8ft **S** 1.2–1.8m/4–6ft

Before the new leaves arrive in spring, this rounded shrub starts producing sweetly fragrant white flower spikes that are largely composed of stamens, little white bottlebrushes. During autumn the bold leaves, 10cm (4in) long, pass through a kaleidoscope of orange, yellow and red colours before they fall. Provide a moist, woodland-type acid soil, enriched with organic matter. Gentle pruning after flowering will keep the size down.

Fothergilla major

Hamamelis vernalis 'Sandra' ♔
Ozark witch hazel

☼ ☼ ❈ ❈ ❈ ♡ **H/S** 2.2m/7ft

Small yellow flowers appear from late winter to early spring, but the main delights of this shrub lie in its magnificent foliage. The leaves are flushed with purple on emerging, but mature to green with purple undersides until the autumn, when they turn incredible colours of rich red, orange and yellow. It grows best in a neutral to acid soil but tolerates chalky soils better than most witch hazels. These plants are propagated commercially by grafting, which tends to make them expensive shrubs to buy.

Hydrangea paniculata 'Pink Diamond'

☼ ☼ ❋ ❋ ❋ ◯

H 1.8–3m /6–10ft **S** 1.5–2.2m /5–7ft

The 30cm (12in) long, pink-flushed flower panicles blend well with other colours of the season and last from late summer right through autumn. For quality flowerheads, a drastic pruning in early spring is recommended, reducing last year's stems to within two or three buds of the previous season's wood; I prefer to thin out older stems every two to three years. Choose a sheltered spot on moist but well-drained soil, enriched with organic matter.

Rosa 'Geranium' (moyesii hybrid) ♛

☼ ❋ ❋ ❋ ◯ **H** 1.8–2.5m /6–8ft **S** 1.5–2.2m /5–7ft

In early summer, on arching branches, this shrubby rose produces bright red single flowers, 5cm (2in) across, with a boss of creamy yellow stamens in the middle. By autumn, these have matured into a lasting crop of elegant, flask-shaped, crimson-orange hips. For a good

Viburnum opulus

set of hips, plant in a moist soil that has been enriched with organic matter and mulch in late winter.

Staphylea pinnata
Bladdernut

☼ ☼ ❋ ❋ ❋ ◯

H 3–4.5m /10–15ft **S** 1.8–2.7m /6–9ft

This underrated shrub has a long season of interest, beginning in late spring with hanging clusters of scented white flowers tinged with pink. These develop into curious, green, bladder-like pods that hang like cocoons from the branches and turn a lovely silvery colour by

PRUNING HEATHERS
❖

Having enjoyed the dried flowers of *Calluna vulgaris* 'Spook' throughout winter, it is time to shear back in spring. Clip over to remove all of the old flower spikes and help keep the plant compact.

19

autumn. For a good set of pods, keep moist in summer. Untidy plants can be renovated by hard pruning in winter.

Viburnum opulus
Guelder rose

☼ ☼ ❋ ❋ ❋ ◯

H 3.7–4.5m /12–15ft **S** 2.7–3.7m /9–12ft

Heads of white lacecap-like flowers appear from late spring to early summer, followed by an autumnal display of opulent, shiny red fruits. At the same time, the maple-like leaves turn from dark green to their orange and red autumn colours. *V.o.* 'Compactum' ♛ suits smaller gardens; for yellow fruits, choose *V.o.* 'Xanthocarpum'. For best results, plant in a moist soil.

◁ **AUTUMN SURPRISES** *Shrubs like* Cotinus coggygria *(left) and* Rhus typhina *'Dissecta' (right) ensure the garden ends its season with an explosion of colour instead of just fading out.*

Shrubs for winter colour

To be able to enjoy flowering shrubs and dazzling stem colours in the depths of winter is a triumph of good planting. Winter blooms tend to be smaller and paler than their summer rivals but they are often sweetly scented. Even when the weather is cold and unwelcoming, sprigs of flowers, and eventually whole sprays, from mature shrubs can be picked to enjoy indoors.

Erica × darleyensis 'Silberschmelze'

20

Abeliophyllum distichum
White forsythia

☀ ❄ ❄ ❄ ◯ **H/S** 1.5m /5ft

This shrub is worth cosseting for its precious display of delicate, fragrant, slightly off-white flowers. Each bears four dainty petals that show up against the stark, leafless stems during late winter and early spring. Site in a sheltered position to protect the blooms from frost, preferably against a warm wall or fence to ripen the wood for flowering.

Acer pensylvanicum 'Erythrocladum' �‸
Moosewood, Striped maple

☀ ☀ ❄ ❄ ❄ ◯ **H/S** 3–4.5m /10–15ft

This shrub is slow to mature but the wait is worthwhile. After the leaves have yellowed and fallen, young shrimp-pink shoots are revealed in all their splendour, maturing to orange-red with typical snakebark white stripes. Plant in a moist, fertile soil, apply controlled-release shrub fertilizer every spring and mulch annually.

Chimonanthus praecox
Wintersweet

☀ ❄ ❄ ❄ ◯ **H** 2.5–3m /8–10ft **S** 1.8–2.5m /6–8ft

This desirable shrub demands patience, as it frequently takes around five years

to establish itself and start flowering. After that, each winter, the reward will be a display of deep yellow, pendent flowers, marked with maroon inside. The sweet, spicy fragrance wafts on the air. Plant where low rays of winter sun can illuminate the blooms.

Cornus sanguinea 'Midwinter Fire'
Dogwood

☀ ❄ ❄ ❄ ◯ **H** 90–120cm /3–4ft **S** 90cm /3ft

This dogwood creeps into the limelight

> #### STOOLING A CORNUS
> ❖
>
> Dogwoods like *Cornus sanguinea* 'Midwinter Fire', grown for its winter stems, need to be cut back in early spring. Remove the previous year's growth to within a short stump of older wood. The stems will then re-grow for next winter.
>
>

during autumn, when its leaves turn a delicate yellow flushed with pinkish-orange before falling quite late to reveal superb stem colours. Glowing orange-yellow stem bases become suffused with reddish-pink towards the tips. Prune all the stems right down to within a bud or two of the older wood at the base every spring.

Erica × darleyensis 'Silberschmelze'
Darley Dale heath

☀ ❄ ❄ ❄ ❧

H 30–38cm /12–15in **S** 45–60cm /18–24in

Winter-flowering heaths and heathers provide first-class flowering ground cover during the colder months. This one opens its white flowers in late autumn and blooms until spring. Both *E.* × *darleyensis*, *E. carnea* and their cultivars will tolerate virtually any soil, including alkaline, provided it is well-drained. Shear off spent flowers in early spring to encourage compact growth.

Hamamelis × intermedia 'Diane' �‸
Witch hazel

☀ ☀ ❄ ❄ ❄ ◯ **H/S** 3–3.7m /10–12ft

With their spidery and fragrant yellow, orange or red flowers, witch hazels brighten up the garden during late winter. *H.* × *intermedia* 'Pallida' �‸ is possibly the classiest and most sweetly fragrant, but 'Diane' bears interesting red flowers and the bonus of bright red and orange autumn tints. Plant in a moist, well-drained, neutral to acid soil.

Lonicera × purpusii 'Winter Beauty' ♈

☼ ☼ ✳ ✳ ✳ ◗ ◐ **H** 2m/6ft **S** 2.5m/8ft

It is possible to have a love–hate relationship with the winter-flowering honeysuckles. On one hand the pale, sweetly fragrant flowers borne in winter and early spring are delightful on the bushes and useful for vases. On the other hand, these climbers are ungainly and space-consuming in summer. They thrive well in most soils and, at most, need only an occasional thinning after flowering.

Rhododendron 'Olive' ♈

☼ ✳ ✳ ✳ ✳ ●

H 90–120cm/3–4ft **S** 75–90cm/30–36in

This early-flowering rhododendron opens its trusses of purple-pink flowers,

---

4cm (1½in) long and wide, in late winter against neat, shiny, dark green leaves. Plant shallowly in moist, well-drained acid soil, away from cold winds and early morning sun. Protect blooms against frost and dead-head straight after flowering. Mulch with leafmould.

Sarcococca hookeriana var. digyna ♈
Christmas box

☼ ✳ ✳ ✳ ✳ ● **H** 1.2m/4ft **S** 1.5m/5ft

The thickets of stems bear elegantly

Viburnum × bodnantense 'Dawn'

tapering leaves which, though they tend to blend into the background during most months of the year, come alive with clusters of small, fragrant white flowers in winter. The sweet scent that is carried on the air seems strangely at odds with such an unassuming, though useful, ground cover shrub. Plant near doorways or along well-used paths to enjoy the benefit of its fragrance. Propagate by taking summer cuttings or removing suckers in winter.

Viburnum × bodnantense 'Dawn' ♈

☼ ☼ ✳ ✳ ✳ ◗

H 2.5–3m/8–10ft **S** 1.8–2.2m/6–7ft

Even if severe frost damages the open flowers, my favourite winter-flowering shrub has plenty more waiting for the next mild spell. The clusters of pink buds, opening to sweetly scented, paler pink tubular flowers, are produced almost continuously from early winter to early spring. Prevent shrubs becoming tall and woody by occasionally thinning out the older stems after flowering.

◁ **ALL WITCH HAZELS BEAR** *fragrant, spidery flowers. Those of* Hamamelis × intermedia *'Diane' are dark red, followed in autumn by bright leaf colours.*

Plants to cover sunny walls

Plants for walls fall into two categories: climbers and wall shrubs. Being specially adapted to cling or twine, climbers are an obvious solution for a vertical surface. Many wall shrubs lend themselves to being trained upwards and tender wall shrubs, as well as climbers, benefit from the shelter offered by a wall that faces the sun most of the day. Its warmth is absorbed by the wall during daytime and given off at night.

22

Solanum crispum

Abutilon vitifolium
☼ ✳ ✳ ◯ **H** 3–4.5m / 10–15ft **S** 2.5–3m / 8–10ft

Choose this hardy abutilon if a wall needs covering quickly. Although not a climber, it requires no support and from late spring to early summer will be covered with saucer-shaped, purplish-blue flowers 8cm (3in) across. The hairy leaves are shaped like those of a maple. Plant in well-drained soil and, if necessary, prune after flowering to curb size. Remove frost-damaged stems in spring.

Actinidia kolomikta ♈
☼ ✳ ✳ ✳ ◯ **H/S** 3.7–5m / 12–16ft

Related to the kiwi fruit, this twining climber is grown for its large, heart-shaped leaves, which take on bizarre colours when young. Their tips become coloured with white and pink as if paint had been splashed on them. Small white flowers are borne during early

Actinidia kolomikta

summer, but they are inconspicuous. Prune back to restrict size if necessary after the colours have faded; new shoots are prone to frost damage.

Buddleja crispa
☼ ✳ ✳ ✳ ◯ **H/S** 2.5–3m / 8–10ft

The stems and leaves, covered by dense white felt, are easily to train against a wall. They provide an ideal silvery backdrop to the panicles of scented, orange-throated lilac flowers that open during mid-to late summer. Plant in well-drained soil and provide shelter. Prune in spring by reducing the length of side shoots that flowered the previous year.

Cytisus battandieri ♈
Pineapple broom/Moroccan broom
☼ ✳ ✳ ✳ ◯ **H/S** 3.7–4.5m / 12–15ft

This delightful shrub is easy to train against a high wall or fence. Tie in the long stems that bear handsome, silvery trifoliate leaves, pruning out any that are unwanted after flowering. Within a year or two, young plants should produce

▷ **FOR A FAST-GROWING SHRUB** *in a warm, sunny position, choose* Cytisus battandieri.

showy, upright candles of yellow, pea-like, pineapple-scented flowers from early to midsummer. Plant in poor, well-drained soil and avoid disturbance.

Piptanthus nepalensis
Evergreen laburnum
☼ ☼ ✳ ✳ ◯ **H** 2.5m / 8ft **S** 1.8m / 6ft

This striking shrub thrives against a sheltered wall if planted in well-drained soil; stems can be trained in when young. Laburnum-like leaflets are dark bluish-green above and blue-white beneath, an effect that contrasts well with the dark green stems. Yellow, pea-like flowers appear during late spring and early summer. Thin by removing the older and weaker stems of mature specimens every year or two after flowering. Propagate by seed sown in spring or basal cuttings in summer.

WALL PLANTING

❖

Thoroughly improve the soil and soak the area prior to digging the planting hole, which should be at least 30cm (12in) away from the wall. Soak the rootball of the new plant and tease out congested roots before planting. Make sure young plants receive adequate water while establishing. Soil at the foot of a wall is often in a rain shadow, remaining dry even when the rest of the garden is moist.

UNUSUAL PLANTS FOR SUNNY WALLS

❖

Acacia dealbata ♀ ●
Ceanothus impressus ♀ ●
Eriobotrya japonica ♀ ●
Fremontodendron 'California Glory' ♀ ●
Jasminum officinale ♀ ○●
Mutisia oligodon ●
Rhamnus alaternus
'Argenteovariegata' ♀ ●
Ribes speciosum ♀ ●

23

Robinia hispida ♀
Rose acacia

☼ ❄ ❄ ❄ ○ **H** 2.5–3.7m /8–12ft **S** 2.5m /8ft

A showy wall shrub, this one starts flowering at a younger stage than most wisterias, producing bunches of showy, pink, pea-like flowers in early summer. The foliage produces a delightful effect with its light green, oval leaflets, whose midribs extend just beyond the blade. Mature shoots are covered with bristles and are rather brittle. Thrives on poor soils but needs shelter from cold winds.

Rosa banksiae var. banksiae 'Lutea' ♀
Yellow Banksian rose

☼ ❄ ❄ ❄ ❄ ● **H** 6m /20ft **S** 3.7m /12ft

This classic, slightly tender rose is ideal for training up a sheltered house wall. Although slow to establish, the wait is rewarded by a distinguished display of delicately fragrant, soft yellow, double flowers in late spring. Held in sprays, the small individual blooms are profuse, so they almost cover the plant. Prune flowered shoots back to within a few buds of the framework after flowering.

Rosa 'Madame Grégoire Staechelin' ♀

☼ ❄ ❄ ❄ ❄ ● **H** 3.7–6m /12–20ft **S** 2.5–3.7m /8–12ft

Choose this superb rose for a high, sunny wall. Its handsome, dark green, glossy foliage is joined by a display of sumptuous, fully double, rounded pink flowers, which hang down slightly. Although there is no repeat flowering, there will be a display of rounded red hips. Prune back to within small spurs of the framework in autumn or spring.

Solanum crispum 'Glasnevin' ♀
Chilean potato vine

☼ ❄ ❄ ❄ ❄ ● **H** 2.5–4.5m /8–15ft **S** 2.5m /8ft

This vigorous shrub is ideal for covering a wall, to which it can be loosely trained. Try it with *Abutilon* x *suntense*, so they provide a mass of purple together, though the solanum opens its starry, yellow-centred blooms all summer, continuing long after the abutilon has finished. Plant in well-drained soil and prune after flowering if necessary.

Wisteria sinensis ♀
Chinese wisteria

☼ ☼ ❄ ❄ ❄ ○ **H** 2.5–6m /8–20ft **S** 2.5–4.5m /8–15ft

Probably the most desirable of climbers, wisterias can be wall-trained by tying in a framework of growths laterally, espalier fashion. Shorten the main shoots by half in winter while establishing, then prune laterals to 25cm (10in) each summer and to two or three buds in winter. Enjoy the rather fleeting late-spring display of fragrant, lilac-blue racemes of flowers.

Piptanthus nepalensis   **Wisteria sinensis**

Plants for shady walls

Some plants not only tolerate a shady position, but thrive better in one. In a garden that receives a lot of sun elsewhere, a stretch of cold wall or fence can be a positive boon, offering plants shade and a cool root run. The following climbers and wall shrubs can then be used as a backdrop for other ornamental shrubs that prefer cool shade in summer, like rhododendron and hydrangea.

24

FIXING TO WALLS

❖

Some climbers and most wall shrubs need tying or training to their supporting wall or fence as they grow. Parallel, horizontal wires stretched tight between two eyes about 60cm (2ft) apart work well, while trellis is both attractive and effective. A simple solution is to tap masonry nails into the mortar between bricks where needed and tie stems individually to these.

Azara microphylla ♔
☼ ☀ ❋ ❋ ❋ ❦ **H** 3m /10ft **S** 2.2m /7ft

Although it is the hardiest of its tribe, this shrub or small tree from Chile and Argentina will still thrive best when given the shelter of a wall. Small, shiny, neatly arranged dark green leaves are joined in late winter and spring by small, vanilla-scented yellow flowers, composed mainly of stamens. Plant in well-drained soil, enriched with organic matter.

Camellia japonica 'Alba Plena'
☼ ❋ ❋ ❋ ❦ **H** 3m /10ft **S** 1.8m /6ft

Cultivars of *Camellia japonica* can reach greater dimensions than predicted, but are easily controlled by pruning. The small, formal, double white flowers of this cultivar open in early spring and should be protected from frosts. Prune back unwanted and outward-facing shoots after flowering. Keep moist during summer, when the flower buds set. Scale insects can be a problem if unchecked, causing sooty mould. Plant in acid soil, enriched with organic matter.

Hedera helix 'Oro di Bogliasco'

Chaenomeles speciosa 'Moerloosii' ♔
Japanese quince, Japonica
☼ ☀ ❋ ❋ ❋ ○ **H/S** 2.5m /8ft

Train the stems of this spreading shrub into a fan shape against a wall or fence. With clusters of flowers the colour of apple blossom, it is guaranteed to brighten a gloomy wall during early and mid-spring. After flowering, prune back unwanted, outward-facing shoots to within three buds of the older framework.

Hedera helix
'Oro di Bogliasco' **Ivy**
☼ ❋ ❋ ❋ ❦ **H** 6m /20ft **S** 3.7m /12ft

Although slow to establish, a young plant of this excellent ivy will begin to climb in earnest some three years after being planted. Clinging with stem roots, it never looks back, producing masses of bright green leaves, each marked with a central gold splash. Eventually, the growth will need curbing annually, usually in late winter. Bryobia mites can cause speckling.

◁ **VIRGINIA CREEPER** (Parthenocissus quinquefolia) *can be relied on to light up a wall or fence with its brilliant autumn colour.*

Jasminum nudiflorum ♀
Winter jasmine
☼ ☼ ✳ ✳ ✳ ⟳ **H/S** 3m /10ft
Deserving of its popularity, winter jasmine is a reliable performer and easy to grow. Plant at least one for a profusion of cheerful yellow flowers borne during the depths of winter against bright green stems. Train in new stems after flowering, then prune out the old and unwanted stems as well as shortening laterals to three or four buds.

Parthenocissus quinquefolia ♀
Virginia creeper
☼ ☼ ✳ ✳ ✳ ⟳ **H/S** 15m /50ft
The hanging stems of this climber are furnished with leaves composed of five leaflets 10cm (4in) long. The stems drape down from the established framework, which anchors itself by means of tendrils armed with disc-like suckers. The autumn finale is a display of brilliant red and purple tints before leaf-fall. Insignificant summer flowers turn into attractive blue-black fruits that birds love. Prune back in winter and train in the framework stems where needed.

Pileostegia viburnoides ♀
☼ ☼ ✳ ✳ ✳ ♠ **H** 6m /20ft **S** 3.7m /12ft
There are few self-clinging evergreen climbers for shady walls, which makes this plant especially desirable. The disadvantage is that it takes a few years to establish and flower well. But the panicles of small, creamy-white flowers eventually make a good late-summer show against the long, leathery leaves. Mature plants layer themselves freely.

Prunus cerasus 'Morello' ♀
Morello cherry
☼ ✳ ✳ ✳ ⟳ **H/S** 2.2m /7ft
A fan-trained morello is attractive, edible, self-fertile and easy to protect from frost and birds. It takes about four years for the stems to form a fan. Thereafter, thin out new growths in spring, leaving one behind each fruiting lateral. After harvesting in late summer, cut back the fruited laterals, leaving the newer shoots to bear next year's crop.

Pyracantha 'Mohave'
Firethorn
☼ ☼ ✳ ✳ ✳ ♠ **H** 4m /12ft **S** 5m /15ft
Neat-growing firethorns may be trained formally or informally against walls. They can make trim moustaches under windows or form parallel tiers up house walls. Look forward to their white, early-summer blossom, followed by a crop of bright red berries lasting into winter. Shorten laterals after flowering, leaving the developing berries in place. Tidy in spring by removing old fruit trusses.

25

Pileostegia viburnoides

Hydrangea anomala

Hydrangea anomala subsp. *petiolaris* ♀
Climbing hydrangea
☼ ☼ ✳ ✳ ✳ ⟳ **H/S** 7.5m /25ft
A classic choice for a shady wall, this climber needs space. Its attractive foliage makes a good foil for the airy white flowerheads produced in summer. These consist of central female flowers, with a constellation of larger sterile flowers around the perimeter. The stems, which cling to a wall with aerial roots, can be cut back to restrict size immediately after flowering.

Plants to cover fences

Fences make good instant boundaries for a garden but they can look rather stark. The answer is to smother them with climbers or wall shrubs, bearing in mind they may need to be pulled away from the fence periodically for maintenance purposes. Many of the climbers described on the preceding pages are also suitable for growing against fences. Do not overlook annuals such as canary creeper and sweet peas.

Passiflora caerulea

26

Ampelopsis glandulosa var. brevipedunculata 'Elegans'
☼ ❋❋❋ ◯ **H/S** 1.2m/4ft

This dainty vine, grown for its mottled foliage of pink and cream over green, clings to its support by means of twining tendrils. The flowers are insignificant but can be followed by a crop of berries that turn from pinkish-purple to blue. Trim back in spring if necessary and, for fence maintenance, cut back hard. Plant in well-drained soil.

Cotoneaster horizontalis ♈
Herringbone cotoneaster
☼ ☼ ❋❋❋❋ ◯ **H** 1.2m/4ft **S** 1.5m/5ft

By nature a ground-covering plant, this shrub also grows upwards to decorate a fence with stems of neat, deep green leaves arranged fishbone-fashion. Small,

pink-tinged white flowers open in spring, followed by a profusion of red fruits that persist even after the leaves have turned red and, by midwinter, have fallen. Plant with winter jasmine for a stunning effect. Prop away from the fence for maintenance purposes. Tolerates a dry spot.

Euonymus fortunei 'Silver Queen' ♈
☼ ☼ ❋❋❋❋ ● **H** 3m/10ft **S** 1.2m/4ft

When offered the support of a fence or other structure, this handsome, evergreen shrub takes on a climbing habit. Its leathery, oval leaves bear irregular margins of creamy white, which show up well against a dark background and take on a pinkish tinge in cold weather. Prop growth away from the fence to carry out maintenance.

Geranium 'Ann Folkard'
☼ ☼ ❋❋❋❋ ◯ **H** 60cm/2ft **S** 1m/3ft

I find this scrambling, herbaceous geranium extremely useful to plug gaps between existing fence plants and tie them together with its growth. It not only sends its wispy stems of yellow-green leaves in all directions but brightens the area with a long season of saucer-shaped magenta flowers, from midsummer to mid-autumn. Cuttings root easily in water or compost.

Lathyrus latifolius ♈
Everlasting pea
☼ ☼ ❋❋❋❋ ◯ **H** 1.8m/6ft **S** 1.5m/5ft

With pink or purple flowers packed closely like clusters of sea-shells, this perennial relative of the sweet pea is such a good climber. Plants romp up trellis in spring and early autumn, after which they die back for winter. *L. l.* 'White Pearl' ♈ bears superb white flowers. Plants tolerate poor soil and some dryness at the roots better than sweet peas do but, sadly, they are unscented.

Lonicera japonica 'Halliana' ♈
Japanese honeysuckle
☼ ☼ ❋❋❋ ●◐ **H** 4.5m/15ft **S** 3m/10ft

A fence will completely disappear under the abundance of Japanese honeysuckle.

Cotoneaster horizontalis

Lathyrus latifolius

Lonicera japonica 'Halliana'

△ ROSA 'CLIMBING ICEBERG' will decorate a fence with its clusters of double white flowers.

PRUNING A RUBUS
❖

The ghostly stems of *Rubus cockburnianus* Golden Vale look wonderful trained against a fence. To prevent it from forming a tangled thicket, prune to thin out the stems in early spring. Older stems can be removed completely every so often by cutting them close to the base. Replace by tying in fresh new stems.

Twining stems with paired oval leaves need initial support, then cling to themselves. White flowers, which age to butter-yellow, appear from spring to late summer, scenting the air for some distance. For maintenance, cut the plant back or replant with a rooted layer.

Passiflora caerulea ♀
Blue passion flower
☼ ◑ ✽ ✽ ✿ **H/S** 4.5m /15ft

There are few more exotic climbers than this tough passion flower, which opens its flowers during summer. The coronas are blue and white, like colourful sea anemones. The orange fruits are decorative but, though edible, are dry and unpalatable. Plant in poor, well-drained soil and offer initial support for the tendril-clad stems. Prune to tidy in spring and cut back for fence maintenance.

Rosa 'Climbing Iceberg' ♀
☼ ✽ ✽ ✽ ✿✿ **H/S** 3m /10ft

The pleasant, light green foliage of this rose is complemented by clusters of double white flowers from summer to autumn. Prune during autumn in milder regions, which tidies the rose for winter, otherwise prune in early spring. Tie strong stems to the fence to create a framework, then shorten lateral growths to short spurs. Loosen ties and lay the rose down from the fence for the purposes of maintenance.

Rosa 'Paul's Scarlet Climber'
☼ ◑ ✽ ✽ ✽ ✿✿ **H** 3m /10ft **S** 2.5m /8ft

This rose blooms only once in summer but becomes smothered by semi-double scarlet flowers held in clusters; it makes an ideal fence partner for 'Climbing Iceberg'. Neither has much fragrance, but visual impact is more important at

the back of a border, against a fence. A tough rose, it will tolerate poor soils. Prune as for 'Climbing Iceberg' (*above*).

Rubus cockburnianus Golden Vale
Whitewashed bramble
☼ ✽ ✽ ✽ ✿ **H/S** 1.2–1.8m /4–6ft

This easy shrub performs well all year. From spring to autumn, the prickly stems are clothed in golden-yellow, fern-like leaves. These drop in autumn to reveal ghostly white stems that make an outstanding feature all winter. Prune in early spring, either by cutting all stems close to the ground or, to retain height, by thinning out only weak and unwanted stems. Prop away from the fence for maintenance.

KEY: ♀ *Award of Merit* ☼ *sun* ◑ *semi-shade* ● *shade* ✽ *half-hardy* ✽✽ *frost-hardy* ✽✽✽ *fully hardy* ✿ *deciduous* ● *evergreen* ✿ *semi-evergreen* **H** *height* **S** *spread*

Climbing plants for arches and pergolas

Arches and pergolas form vertical structures in the garden and make great climbing frames for plants that cling and climb. Make sure they are in scale with the house and garden; a pergola of generous proportions means plenty of space for larger climbers. Provide initial support and training, then watch them romp away.

28

Akebia quinata
Chocolate vine

☼ ☼ ✳ ✳ ✳ ❀ **H/S** 2.5–6m/8–20ft

Peeping between fresh green leaflets in spring are the small but unusual flowers of this interesting twiner. Each consists of three dark maroon-purple sepals and

gives off a perfume reminiscent of vanilla, spice and possibly milk chocolate. In good light, mature plants may set peculiar purplish, sausage-shaped fruits. Allow plants to romp on a pergola, pruning after flowering to restrict their size if necessary.

Akebia quinata

Eccremocarpus scaber ♔
Chilean glory flower

☼ ✳ ✳ ❧ **H** 1.2–3m/4–10ft **S** 1–1.5m/3–5ft

Easily raised from spring-sown seed, these cheerful, leaf-tendril climbers can be treated as annuals or, in milder regions, as perennials. They open their tubular red flowers with orange throats from early summer to the autumn; seed mixtures with pink or yellow flowers are also available. For best results, plant in fertile, well-drained soil.

Holboellia coriacea

☼ ☼ ✳ ✳ ✳ ❀ **H/S** 2.5–6m/8–20ft

Closely related and possibly muddled with the genus *Stauntonia*, this species is the hardiest of the bunch. A twining climber, it bears attractive foliage and spring flowers that are distinctly male or female. The male flowers, flushed with purple, are borne in terminal clusters, while the females are more greenish-white and occur in axillary clusters. Sausage-like purple fruits may follow. Prune as for Akebia (*above*).

Humulus lupulus 'Aureus' ♔
Golden hop

☼ ☼ ✳ ✳ ✳ ♡ **H/S** 3–5m/10–16ft

This deciduous, twining hop is ideal for an arch or pergola required to provide shade during summer but allow light through during winter. Its herbaceous stems, furnished with beautifully lobed, golden-yellow leaves, climb up their supports during summer, then die back for winter. Plant in a sunny position to bring out the best leaf colours. Provide a moist, fertile soil.

Lonicera periclymenum 'Serotina'

Lonicera periclymenum 'Serotina' ♔
Late Dutch honeysuckle

☼ ☼ ☼ ✳ ✳ ✳ ✳ ♡

H 3.7–6m/12–20ft **S** 3.7m/12ft

Honeysuckles are well represented in early summer, but choose this one to prolong the succession of blooms and sweet, fruity fragrance into late summer and autumn. Reddish-purple buds open to white flowers streaked pinkish-purple. Blooms can be prone to aphid attack: either spray with insecticide or encourage birds into the garden. Shorten stems in early spring.

Rosa 'Compassion' ♔

☼ ✳ ✳ ✳ ✳ ❀

H 3m/10ft **S** 2.5m/8ft

The exquisitely formed buds of this modern rose open into generous, double flowers of delicate salmon-pink, flushed with mango towards the centre. Fully unfurled,

△ **ALLOW CLIMBERS** *their freedom but stop plants like golden hop from swamping roses.*

they reveal a boss of golden stamens. The fragrance is full and fruity. Tie stems in to their supports and dead-head assiduously to ensure the best flowers from summer to autumn. Prune in late autumn or early spring.

Rosa 'Félicité Perpétue' ♀
☼ ☀ ✳ ✳ ✳ ● **H** 4.5m /15ft **S** 3.7m /12ft
This pretty old rambler flowers in late summer, after the main flushes of other roses. The build-up begins with small red buds and climaxes as each opens into a rosette of creamy-white petals. Other attributes are scent and glossy foliage. Prune only lightly in late summer.

Tropaeolum peregrinum
Canary creeper
☼ ✳ **H** 1.5–2.5m /5–8ft **S** 90cm–1.8m /3–6ft
Quick gap-fillers are useful to clothe new structures and plug temporary holes where old plants have died. Sow this

Vitis coignetiae

climbing annual in late winter or early spring under glass, to plant out as soon as danger of frost has passed. All summer and into autumn, it produces masses of foliage and bright yellow, spurred and fringed flowers, resembling small birds.

Vitis coignetiae ♀
Crimson glory vine
☼ ☀ ✳ ✳ ✳ **H/S** 4.5–15m /15–50ft
The large, roughly heart-shaped leaves, 30cm (12in) long, of this stupendous vine are lush and green during summer, but are grown mainly for the effect of their magnificent yellow, orange, red and purple leaf colours in autumn. Plant only on large pergolas and stand back. Prune hard during winter. Avoid cutting into mature wood during summer.

Wisteria floribunda 'Multijuga' ♀
Japanese wisteria
☼ ☀ ✳ ✳ ✳ ○ **H/S** 9m /30ft
The queen of wisterias produces tapering racemes 30cm (12in) or more long, of fragrant, mauve-blue and white flowers in early summer. Pergolas allow wisterias to grow with their wild, tree-climbing habit. Retain control by shortening the laterals to four to six leaves in summer and to within two or three buds of the older framework in winter.

29

CLIMBING COMPANIONS FOR PERGOLAS
❖

Clematis alpina ♀ ○
Clematis 'Bill MacKenzie' ♀ ○
Lonicera x *brownii*
'Dropmore Scarlet' ●
Lonicera x *italica* ○
Lonicera periclymenum 'Belgica' ♀ ○
Lonicera periclymenum
'Graham Thomas' ♀ ○
Rosa 'Madame Alfred Carrière' ♀ ●
Tropaeolum tuberosum var.
lineamaculatum 'Ken Aslet' ♀ ○

PRUNING AND TRAINING
❖

I usually find it necessary to tackle the pergola about three times a year. In spring, it is the turn of roses to be pruned and tied in thoroughly. This must be achieved without harming the dead-looking stems of *Clematis alpina*, soon to produce its display of attractive blue flowers. The early summer-flowering honeysuckle, *Lonicera* x *italica*, is pruned as soon as it has finished and the roses will need some taming in late summer.

Ground cover plants

These valuable, mostly herbaceous plants provide breathing spaces between other subjects, at the same time as suppressing weed growth and shading the soil from sun. Many are beautiful in their own right but together make good ground cover when they knit together above ground and provide a mass of roots below.

Lamium maculatum 'Pink Nancy'

---

30 *Alchemilla mollis* ♔

Lady's mantle

☀ ☼ ❄ ❄ ❄ ○

H 45–60cm /18–24in **S** 60–75cm /24–30in

The soft, rounded leaves with lobed and toothed edges look divine when beaded with moisture. Tiny, greenish-yellow flowers are individually beautiful and make a soft haze over the plant in early to midsummer. Easy and drought-tolerant, one plant quickly makes a clump large enough to be lifted, divided and replanted during spring or autumn. These perennials also seed themselves around.

Bergenia 'Sunningdale'

Elephant's ears

☀ ☼ ❄ ❄ ❄ ●

H 30–45cm /12–18in **S** 45–60cm /18–24in

With their bold, leathery, evergreen foliage, bergenias make ideal year-round ground cover for a more formal area, such as a small north-facing town garden. This form boasts deep green leaves with red undersides, which turn bronzy-red

Bergenia 'Sunningdale'

during winter. Red stems bearing lilac-pink flowers rise up in spring. Lift, divide and replant in groups during autumn or spring.

Corydalis cheilanthifolia

☀ ☼ ❄ ❄ ❄ ● **H/S** 30cm /12in

These tough perennials make elegant clumps of fern-like foliage, which turns bronze-coloured during cold snaps. Racemes of dainty yellow flowers are produced from spring to early summer. Resilient plants, they colonize well and seed themselves into unprepossessing cracks and crevices. Remove old leaves after winter frosts. Lift, divide and replant in autumn, choosing well-drained soil.

Cotoneaster salicifolius 'Gnom'

☀ ☼ ❄ ❄ ❄ ●

H 23–30cm /9–12in **S** 90–150cm /3–5ft

Capable of providing dense, evergreen cover, this low-growing shrub bears arching purple stems of narrow, dark green leaves 2.5cm (1in) long, which turn an attractive bronze in winter. In good light, the small white flowers, borne in early summer, will be followed by a reasonable crop of small red berries. Tolerates dry conditions and is useful for covering banks.

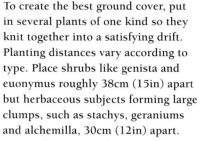

SPACING PLANTS

To create the best ground cover, put in several plants of one kind so they knit together into a satisfying drift. Planting distances vary according to type. Place shrubs like genista and euonymus roughly 38cm (15in) apart but herbaceous subjects forming large clumps, such as stachys, geraniums and alchemilla, 30cm (12in) apart. Set small portions of creeping plants, like lamium and bugle (*Ajuga*), 20cm (8in) apart. Plant bulbs like alliums and narcissus among them.

Epimedium pinnatum subsp. *colchicum* ♔

Barrenwort, Bishop's mitre

☼ ❄ ❄ ❄ ● **H** 30–38cm /12–15in **S** 25cm /10in

The epimediums have beautiful tooth-edged leaves and flourish in shade; this one makes excellent ground cover and bears yellow flowers with dark centres in late spring. Try cutting the old leaves back in early spring to show off the flowers. The new foliage is bronze-tinted. Lift and divide into small portions in autumn or after flowering, and replant.

Genista lydia ♔

Broom

☀ ❄ ❄ ❄ ○ **H** 30–60cm /12–24in **S** 60–90cm /2–3ft

Even when not in flower, the mass of bright green, almost leafless stems of this small shrub forms dense, structural

◁ **LADY'S MANTLE** (Alchemilla mollis) *makes good-value ground cover from spring right through to autumn. Even when dormant, its root-mass leaves no room for weeds.*

Stachys macrantha 'Superba'

☼ ☀ ✳ ✳ ✳ ● H 60cm/2ft S 30cm/12in

In addition to covering the soil well, this stachys is a good flowering plant that associates well with silver-leaved species as well as old roses. Rosettes of dark, hairy leaves rise up to produce spikes of rich, purple-pink flowers in early summer; these continue to bloom on and off until autumn. Plant in good, moist soil. Remove rooted sections to make more clumps.

Tiarella cordifolia ♀
Foam flower

☼ ☀ ✳ ✳ ✳ ● H 15–30cm/6–12in S 30cm/12in

An understated but successful ground cover is provided by foam flower's presentable, roughly heart-shaped leaves, which become flushed with bronze in autumn. During summer, they are enlivened by foam-like heads of fluffy white flowers. Running roots ensure a good knitting together against weeds. Plant in reasonably moist soil for best results. Divide and replant in spring.

---

mounds. In early summer a profusion of yellow, pea-like flowers opens. Plant in well-drained soil that is not too rich and plants will suppress weeds and tolerate drought. Take semi-ripe cuttings in summer.

Geranium macrorrhizum
Balkan cranesbill

☼ ☀ ✿ ✳ ✳ ✳ ✿

H 38–50cm/15–20in S 60cm/2ft

The mounds of well-shaped, aromatic leaves soon knit together to provide a seamless, weed-suppressing ground cover. They turn reddish in autumn, colouring up best when grown on poor soil. Pink flowers are produced in early summer. Those of *G.m.* 'Ingwersen's Variety' ♀ are particularly choice, being pale pink over light green foliage. Lift, divide and replant in autumn or spring.

Lamium maculatum 'White Nancy' ♀

☼ ✳ ✳ ✳ ● H 8–15cm/3–6in S 30–90cm/1–3ft

For mats of spreading cover, this lamium is hard to beat. A carpet of silvery leaves, each with a narrow green margin, are brightened by white flowers in summer. Non-flowering side shoots are easy to root, even in water. Leaves are liable to scorch in hot sun. *L.m.* 'Pink Nancy' is equally useful and bears pink flowers.

Geranium macrorrhizum

Stachys macrantha

Tiarella cordifolia

KEY: ♀ *Award of Merit* ☼ *sun* ☀ *semi-shade* ✿ *shade* ✳ *half-hardy* ✳✳ *frost-hardy* ✳✳✳ *fully hardy* ✐ *deciduous* ● *evergreen* ✐ *semi-evergreen* **H** *height* **S** *spread*

Cottage garden plants

The cottage garden style has been popular ever since the idea of gardens evolved. Our modern-day equivalent may well be a romanticized version of the subsistence plots of old, but it relies on a fulsome planting of flowering annuals and perennials, rich with colour and variety. At its best at the height of summer, with its jumble of flowers and bright colours, the cottage style has seductive charm.

Iris 'Jane Phillips'

32

Achillea filipendulina 'Gold Plate' ♈
Yarrow

☼ ❉ ❉ ❉ ▰ **H** 1.2m /4ft **S** 75cm /30in

Slightly domed heads, packed full of small, golden-yellow flowers, seem to hover over the leaves of this tall perennial from summer to early autumn. Choose a roomy site and rig up some support early in the season, otherwise the stems, though strong, can collapse. Combines well with silver, blue and purple flowers. Lift, divide and replant old clumps in early spring.

Alcea rosea Chater's Double Group
Hollyhock

☼ ❉ ❉ ❉ ♂ **H** 2–2.5m /6–8ft **S** 60cm /2ft

Although perennial, hollyhocks are usually treated as biennials. Seed is sown in spring, to plant in autumn for flowers the following summer. Widely grown in the mid-1800s, hollyhocks were almost wiped out by rust disease. There are single and double-flowered cultivars from which to choose.

Alcea rosea
(semi-double)

SUPPORTING PLANTS

❖

A very natural way of supporting lax-stemmed plants like ox-eye daisies is to save twiggy prunings. Pushed into the soil and angled towards the stems, they are unobtrusive and flexible.

This peony-flowered seed strain is a remnant from the old Saffron Walden seed firm of Chater and includes reds, yellows and maroons. Plant in fertile soil for the best results. Strong plants usually survive despite rust.

Delphinium 'Faust' ♈

☼ ❉ ❉ ❉ ♂ **H** 1.8m /6ft **S** 60cm /2ft

To grow the best delphiniums, first select good named varieties. These distinguish themselves by producing spires of closely arranged summer flowers, with the topmost buds opening

---

CREATING THE COTTAGE GARDEN STYLE

❖

- Set strong shapes in the bones of the garden, then use informal plants to create billowing borders. Arches and bowers create a romantic scene.

- Colonize the soil beneath roses with thyme, viola, stachys and gypsophila.

- Include some plants with spires of flowers, like foxglove, lupin, hollyhock and delphinium.

- Edge paths with catmint or lavender; do not be afraid to use repetition.

- Introduce self-seeders such as aquilegia, sweet rocket, *Lychnis coronaria* and Shirley poppies.

---

before the lowest flowers start to age. 'Faust' bears semi-double blue, purple-shaded flowers with dark eyes. Thin the developing shoots to three or four in spring, taking the remainder as cuttings. Protect from slugs all year round and support the flower spikes. Plant in well-conditioned soil and keep moist.

Gypsophila paniculata
Baby's breath

☼ ❉ ❉ ❉ ♂

H 75cm–1.2m /30–48in **S** 90–120cm /3–4ft

This pretty, airy perennial associates well

◁ **THE RIGHT INGREDIENTS,** *like spire-forming verbascum, centaurea, calendula, leucanthemum, phlox and* Lychnis chalcedonica, *produce a romantic cottage garden profusion.*

strain can be maintained by allowing only the best to seed. They fit ideally into an informal, cottage garden style.

Rosa 'Cornelia' ♔
☼ ☽ ❊ ❊ ❊ *◐* **H/S** 1.5m /5ft

Although a modern shrub rose, this one is in keeping with a cottage garden philosophy. Flowering reliably over a long period, it bears sprays of highly fragrant, soft pink flowers, suffused with warm apricot. Buds are more intensely coloured than open blooms, giving a range of shades. Prune lightly in early spring.

33

with most plants, including roses. Blooms rising through the froth of tiny white flowers transform the combination into an instant bouquet. Linear leaves build up quietly during spring, before the flowers burst forth in summer. Plant in light, preferably alkaline, well-drained soil as they can be killed by winter waterlogging.

Iris 'Jane Phillips' ♔
Bearded iris
☼ ☽ ❊ ❊ ❊ *◐* **H/S** 90cm /3ft

Popular and widely available, this lovely, tall iris bears clear, sky-blue flowers. Sniff into the blooms for their sweet scent, which is reminiscent of cheap sweets or old-fashioned soap. Their structural, sword-shaped leaves bring form to riotous borders. When the clumps become congested, lift, cut off the healthy outer growths, shorten the leaves and replant into well-drained soil after flowering or in early autumn.

Lychnis coronaria
Dusty miller, Rose campion
☼ ☽ ❊ ❊ ❊ *●* **H** 60–80cm /24–32in **S** 45cm /18in

The dusty miller can withstand drought and malnutrition, but not dampness in the air or at the roots. Under the right conditions, it will form colonies of silver-

felted basal leaves and stems of shocking pink summer flowers. I prefer the more refined white-flowered form, *L.c.* Alba Group ♔ with a soft pink eye. Both seed themselves with abandon or you can divide and replant in spring.

Nepeta 'Six Hills Giant'
Catmint
☼ ❊ ❊ ❊ *◐* **H/S** 90cm /3ft

Billowing clumps of aromatic catmint are very reminiscent of cottage gardens. Tiny, lavender-blue flowers open against narrow, toothed, grey-green leaves and attract both bees and cats. If you cut back after the first exuberant flush, fresh growth will result. Plant in well-drained soil. Take summer cuttings and look out for natural layers.

Papaver rhoeas Shirley Series
Shirley poppy
☼ ❊ ❊ ❊ *◐* **H** 60–90cm /2–3ft **S** 45cm /18in

Bred from the common annual cornfield poppy in a process of selection by the Reverend W. Wilks in Shirley, Croydon, these lovely poppies date from 1880. Their silky flowers are single with a white base, yellow or white stamens and no black markings. Once sown, the

Lychnis coronaria   *Nepeta* 'Six Hills Giant'

Salvia × *sylvestris* 'Mainacht' ♔
☼ ❊ ❊ ❊ *◐*

H 70cm /28in **S** 45cm /18in

Erect spikes of deep indigo-blue flowers rise up on this clump-forming perennial during early and midsummer, contrasting well with silver, pink and yellow colours in the border. The mid-green leaves are attractively scalloped and covered in soft hairs. Plant in good, moist, but well-drained soil. Lift, divide and replant older clumps in autumn or spring.

KEY: ♔ *Award of Merit* ☼ *sun* ☽ *semi-shade* ● *shade* ❊ *half-hardy* ❊❊ *frost-hardy* ❊❊❊ *fully hardy* *◐ deciduous* *● evergreen* *◑ semi-evergreen* **H** *height* **S** *spread*

Architectural plants

Using plants for the architectural effect of their foliage is like selecting pieces of living sculpture to act as focal points in the garden. Bold shapes are important in gardens, so that some plants become distinct from masses of small leaves and flowers. Filling a whole garden with structural plants will create a tropical or Mediterranean atmosphere: include large-leaved eucalypts and tender subjects like canna, banana and ricinus.

Arundo donax
Giant reed

☼ ❄ ❄ 🍃 **H** 5m /15ft **S** 1.5m /5ft

Use this grass to create a lush jungle-effect, as its tall, reed-like stems, furnished with long, flat leaves, will tower over more ordinary plants. Cut down the old stems in spring to remove frost damage and promote fresh, new growth. But to encourage the production of feathery flower panicles in autumn, leave the stems for two years before pruning. Plant in moist soil. This rhizomatous perennial can be propagated by division.

Astelia chathamica

☼ ☼ ❄ ❄ 🍃 **H** 1.5m /5ft **S** 90cm /3ft

The ghostly, sword-leaved astelias create great impact in sheltered gardens or they can be grown in containers to overwinter under glass. The upper leaf surfaces are silvery green and the undersides silver; sprays of brownish flowers are borne by mature plants. Mine flourish in full sun and poor, sandy, neutral soil, although they are said to prefer a moist, humus-rich, acid soil. Clear away the dead leaves twice yearly. Divide in spring.

Dicksonia antarctica ♀
Soft tree fern

☼ ☼ ❄ ❄ 🍃 **H** 1.2–6m /4–20ft **S** 1.2–3.7m /4–12ft

These desirable and expensive tree ferns lend a tropical, almost prehistoric atmosphere to a garden. In favoured areas, it is worth planting them in sheltered positions. The fronds usually die back for winter and the crowns can be protected by old fronds and dry bracken, covered in hessian. Plant in moist, acid soil enriched by the addition of organic matter and keep the 'trunk' moist. Propagate by sowing fresh spores.

Fatsia japonica ♀
False castor oil plant

☼ ☼ ❄ ❄ 🍂 **H/S** 1.5–3.7m /5–12ft

The imposing, glossy, hand-like leaves of fatsia make it instantly recognizable. Modest specimens can flourish in sheltered courtyards but will grow large and lush in milder gardens where they can be sheltered from cold winter winds. Mature plants produce small white flowers arranged into spherical heads in long umbels, in autumn. Propagate by cuttings in summer or try air layering.

Musa basjoo
Japanese banana

☼ ❄ ❄ 🍃 **H** 2.2–4.5m /7–15ft **S** 1.8–3.7m /6–12ft

Choose a sheltered position for this banana and it will survive surprisingly low temperatures outside. In normal, frosty winters, most growth dies back

Astelia chathamica

Fatsia japonica

Phormium 'Sundowner'

◁ **THE STRIKING** *and colourful Yucca flaccida 'Golden Sword' is a worthy garden plant. Its leaves make a bold rosette, joined by the interesting silhouette of the flower spike.*

Trachycarpus fortunei ♀
Chusan palm

☼ ☼ ✳ ✳ 🍃

H 6–20m /20–70ft **S** 2.5m /8ft

The impatient would be well advised to save up for a mature specimen of this exotic-looking but hardy palm. Mine, taken as a sucker some nine years ago, is still only 1.5m (5ft) tall, with no sign of a trunk. Pleated leaflets are arranged in a fan shape. Plant in well-drained, fertile soil with protection from wind.

Viburnum cinnamomifolium ♀
☼ ☼ ✳ ✳ 🍃 **H/S** 4.5m /15ft

The dark green, leathery, oval leaves of this imposing shrub are marked with three veins running down their length. About 15cm (6in) long, they are attached to their stems by pink-tinged stalks. Small flowers are held in flattish heads during early summer and followed by small, blue-black fruits. Propagate by summer cuttings.

Trachycarpus fortunei

Yucca gloriosa ♀
Adam's needle, Spanish dagger

☼ ✳ ✳ ✳ 🍃 **H/S** 1.5m /5ft

This tough yucca seems able to tolerate drought and disturbance without suffering unduly. My mature plant has a branching trunk boasting two tufts of dangerously pointed, lance-shaped leaves. Spikes of sweetly scented, ivory-coloured, bell-shaped flowers appear most years in late summer, adding another 1.5m (5ft) to its height. Prise away rooted suckers in spring.

Yucca flaccida 'Golden Sword' ♀
☼ ✳ ✳ ✳ 🍃 **H** 60cm /2ft **S** 1.5m /5ft

This plant could not be more different from the yucca described above. The stemless rosette of bright green leaves, marked vertically with a broad stripe of creamy yellow, looks superb against the shingle of a dry garden. The leaf tips are less stiff and pointed and the margins bear curling threads. Panicles of creamy-white flowers, 1.5m (5ft) tall, are borne in late summer. Propagate by suckers in spring.

and should not be removed, as dead leaves insulate the crown. Take off the decayed growth in spring when new shoots arise. Plants can flower and fruit but the small bananas are unpalatable. Plant in rich soil and propagate by seed or rooted suckers.

Phormium 'Sundowner' ♀
New Zealand flax

☼ ✳ ✳ ✳ 🍃 **H/S** 1.5–1.8m /5–6ft

This compact and colourful New Zealand flax has much to recommend it. The sword-shaped leaves have a bronze cast to them and are paler beneath and decorated by irregular pink stripes down their length and along the margins; the odd cream stripe is thrown in for good measure. Plant in well-drained soil and, with dry feet, they survive surprisingly low winter temperatures. Lift, divide and replant in spring.

GROOMING CARE

Architectural plants benefit from regular attention to keep them looking their best. I cut away the dead phormium leaves twice a year.

Scented plants

Scent is a powerful addiction and, once attuned, a gardener will find delicious fragrances at every turn. It took me years to realize that most bearded iris were scented and that Magnolia soulangiana was worth a sniff. Leaves are often aromatic too, but they may need to be brushed or rubbed to release their scent. Dried leaves and petals can be used to make pot-pourri.

Mentha × piperita f. citrata

Cercidiphyllum japonicum ♛
Katsura

☼ ☼ ❋ ❋ ❋ ○ **H** 15m/50ft **S** 10m/33ft

The dying yellow, orange and red leaves of this dainty woodland tree produce the scent of caramel as they fall in autumn. If you rub one, the unexpected aroma of burnt sugar is released. Plant in soil enriched with organic matter, in a sheltered spot because the coppery young leaves are prone to spring frost-damage. Usually grows multi-stemmed unless trained to a single trunk.

Convallaria majalis ♛
Lily-of-the-valley

☼ ☼ ❋ ❋ ❋ ○ **H** 23cm/9in **S** 17cm/7in

Their show might be short-lived, but I really look forward to the arching stems of sweetly scented, white, bell-shaped flowers set against paired leaves. Most gardens have a moist, shaded spot for these perennials to colonize. Within a few years, one or two small plants will have spread to a sizeable mass. Divide and replant rhizomes in autumn.

Dianthus 'Doris' ♛
Modern pink

☼ ❋ ❋ ❋ ◗ **H** 25–45cm/10–18in **S** 40cm/16in

Pinks are excellent for clothing the edges of paths and they like a well-nourished, well-drained, neutral to alkaline soil. 'Doris' is pretty, with scented, double, sugar-pink flowers marked towards the centre with darker pink. The main flush is in early summer, but rigorous dead-heading and a midsummer feed will encourage more blooms. Propagate by summer cuttings.

Lathyrus odoratus ♛
Sweet pea

☼ ❋ ❋ ❋ **H** 1.8m/6ft **S** 90cm/3ft

Among modern-day sweet pea cultivars and mixtures are many sold for their scent. But for something more unusual, with guaranteed perfume, seek out their ancestor for the beauty of its strongly fragrant magenta and purple flowers. Their charm makes up for the lack of long stems and frilly petals. Sow seed of this annual into pots in autumn or spring, planting out later into well-nourished soil, near a support for the stems to climb. Dead-head rigorously to prolong blooms.

Lilium regale ♛
Regal lily

☼ ☼ ❋ ❋ ❋ ○ **H** 60–180cm/2–6ft **S** 30cm/1ft

One of the easiest and least fussy lilies to grow, one bulb quickly builds up into a clump on most soils. As many as 30 white, trumpet-shaped blooms with yellow throats and purple-pink outsides open in summer. Their strong, heady perfume wafts out on the air, particularly during evening. Plant 15cm (6in) deep in spring or, preferably, in autumn.

36

Convallaria majalis

Lathyrus odoratus cv

Magnolia grandiflora 'Exmouth'

◁ AMONG THE MOST SUCCESSFUL *of garden lilies,* Lilium regale *scents the air for some distance. Bulbs settle down quickly, multiplying to form a colony.*

Myrtus communis

BEST FOR FRAGRANCE

❖

Akebia quinata 🍃
Aquilegia fragrans ♡
Chimonanthus praecox ♡
Choisya ternata ♀ 🍃
Clematis heracleifolia var. *davidiana* 'Wyevale' ♀ ♡
Cytisus battandieri ♀ 🍃
Daphne bholua 'Jacqueline Postill' ♀ 🍃
Elaeagnus × *ebbingei* 🍃
Erysimum cheiri cvs. 🍃
Gladiolus callianthus ♀ ♡
Hamamelis × *intermedia* 'Pallida' ♀ ♡
Heliotropium arborescens 🍃
Hosta plantaginea ♡
Lavandula angustifolia 'Twickel Purple' ♀ 🍃
Lonicera japonica 'Halliana' ♀ 🍃
L. periclymenum 'Serotina' ♀ ♡
L. × *purpusii* ♡
Mentha × *piperita* f *citrata* ♡
Philadelphus 'Sybille' ♀ ♡
Rosmarinus officinalis 🍃
Viburnum × *burkwoodii* 'Anne Russell' ♀ 🍃

37

Magnolia grandiflora

☼ ❋ ❋ 🍃 **H** 6–18m /20–60ft **S** 4.5–15m /15–50ft

Worth growing for its 20cm- (8in-) long glossy leaves alone, this evergreen shrub or tree is usually trained against a warm, sunny wall. Large, creamy-white flowers up to 25cm (10in) across have an exotic, citrus perfume and are even more desirable for being sparsely produced from summer to autumn. Choose *M.g.* 'Exmouth' ♀ for its hardiness or *M.g.* 'Goliath' ♀ for its broad leaves and massive blooms. Tolerates alkaline soils.

Myrtus communis ♀
Myrtle

☼ ❋ ❋ 🍃 **H/S** 2–3m /6–10ft

During late summer and early autumn, pink, fist-like buds open to small, creamy-white flowers with prominent stamens. These have a sweet, spicy fragrance that combines well with the bright green, aromatic leaves. A Mediterranean shrub, myrtle enjoys a well-drained soil and will flourish against a sunny, sheltered wall. Strike semi-ripe cuttings in late summer.

Nicotiana alata
Tobacco plant

☼ ☼ ❋ ♡ **H** 90–120cm /3–4ft **S** 60cm /2ft

Greenish-yellow flowers remain closed during the daytime but flare open in the evening, revealing white mouths and filling the air with a powerful, almost too-sweet perfume. Treat as a half-hardy annual, sowing under glass in spring to flower during summer. Leave the plants in and they may reveal their perennial nature by growing back the following spring.

Pelargonium crispum 'Variegatum' ♀
Lemon-scented pelargonium

☼ ❋ 🍃 **H** 45cm /18in **S** 30cm /24in

One of a number of scented-leaved pelargoniums, this, for me, has the nicest lemon perfume. Rub one of the neat, cream-edged leaves gently and a mild, mouthwatering fragrance is released. Pale mauve flowers appear throughout summer. This upright, tender plant needs protection from frost during winter. Propagate from summer cuttings.

Rosa Alec's Red

☼ ❋ ❋ ❋ 🍃 **H** 90–120cm /3–4ft **S** 90cm /3ft

Sinking one's nose into the satiny, warm red petals of this rose on a hot summer's day is a memorable experience. A reliable modern hybrid tea, it produces a succession of large flowers in a voluptuous shade of dark cherry-red. Its rich fragrance is powerful but pleasant. Plant this rose into well-nourished soil. Prune, then feed and mulch the roots annually in early spring.

Decorative seedheads

Growth, development, flowering, fading and seeding are all fascinating stages in a plant's life cycle. Choosing plants that die gracefully and produce long-lasting seedheads adds yet another dimension to the garden. As well as encouraging drifts of pods and seedheads to decorate the garden in autumn, try cutting some seedheads just before the seeds mature, for use in dried-flower arrangements.

Physalis alkekengi

Acanthus spinosus ♈
Bear's breeches

38

☼ ☼ ❄ ❄ ❄ ● **H** 1.2m /4ft **S** 60–90cm /2–3ft

Tall spires of tubular white flowers, peeping from beneath shiny purple bracts, rise up from the clumps of large, deeply cut leaves of this perennial from late spring to midsummer. These dry to papery husks bearing large seeds; leave them on the plant as they look wonderful covered in hoar frost. Sow seed or divide clumps in spring and take root cuttings in winter.

Allium cristophii ♈
Ornamental onion, Star of Persia

☼ ❄ ❄ ❄ ⟳ **H** 30–60cm /1–2ft **S** 20cm /7in

A narrow growth habit means that bulbs can be slotted between and among other plants in the garden during autumn, setting them 15–20cm (6–8in) deep. In early summer, round heads 20cm (8in) across, on tall stems, are packed with starry purple flowers. The flowers fade to leave green, then parchment-coloured seedheads, which persist into winter and which dry well.

Astilboides tabularis
(formerly *Rodgersia tabularis*)

☼ ❄ ❄ ❄ ⟳ **H/S** 90–120cm /3–4ft

Treated to rich, moist soil, the rounded, lobed and softly hairy leaves of this perennial grow tall and lush, joined by panicles of small, creamy-white flowers in early and midsummer. Plant where the slanting rays of late winter sun will catch the fluffy, rounded seedheads and bring them to life. Especially useful for bog or waterside plantings. Lift, divide and replant in spring.

Eryngium giganteum ♈
Miss Willmott's ghost

☼ ❄ ❄ ❄ ⟳ **H** 90–120cm /3–4ft **S** 30–60cm /1–2ft

Toothed, silvery bracts make a ghostly and elaborate collar around each domed umbel of tiny blue flowers. The stems can be cut and dried just before the flowers open in summer. Although a short-lived perennial, this prickly customer is usually treated as a biennial; it self-seeds with abandon. Plant in well-drained soil.

Nigella damascena
Love-in-a-mist

☼ ❄ ❄ ❄ **H** 60–75cm /2–3ft **S** 45cm /18in

Some hardy annuals can be used to provide a unifying theme for garden beds and borders. Simply sow nigella seed into the ground, thin out the seedlings and wait for the blue flowers of varying intensity, each sitting in a ruff of finely divided leaves. These fade to leave inflated capsules with prominent styles. Choose *N.d.* 'Miss Jekyll' for sky-blue flowers on plants 45cm (18in) tall.

Lagurus ovatus
Hare's tail

☼ ❄ ❄ ❄ **H** 50cm /20in **S** 30cm /12in

To give a soft, natural feel to the garden, sow patches of this annual, Mediterranean grass straight into the soil in spring. Narrow, grassy foliage is

Eryngium giganteum

Lagurus ovatus

Papaver somniferum

△ **THE STARRY FLOWERS** *of* Allium cristophii *burst open during early summer, forming magnificent rounded heads.* Nigella damascena *grown from spring sowings are setting their decorative pods.*

COLLECTING SEED

❖

Saving seed from the garden is an economical and excellent method of building up numbers of species to create drifts. Seed from highly bred plants will not come true and should be viewed as experimental only. When collecting from variable annuals and biennials, like some types of poppy, be prepared to rogue out undesirable plants before their pollen influences the rest. Collect pods and capsules into paper bags labelled with the plant name and date. Keep dry until there is time to clean the seed from its husks and pods. Store in paper envelopes in a cool, dry place until you are ready to sow them.

---

joined by a long succession of soft, oval spikelets throughout summer. Green at first, then tinged purple with maturity, they finally bleach to buff as they age. Pick just before maturity for drying.

Papaver orientale
Oriental poppy

☼ ✳ ✳ ✳ ◯ **H** 60–120cm/2–4ft **S** 30cm/12in

The silky petals fall from the blowsy, short-lived flowers of oriental poppies to reveal a seed capsule of great beauty. The top is covered by a cap composed of velvety maroon spokes over a smooth, pale green pod housing the maturing seeds. Plant in fertile, well-drained soil; lift and divide in spring or take root cuttings at virtually any time.

Physalis alkekengi ♀
Chinese lantern

☼ ☼ ✳ ✳ ✳ ◯ **H** 60cm/2ft **S** 60–90cm/2–3ft

Surreal, bright orange, lantern-like calyces develop during late summer from creamy-white flowers. Papery in

---

SILKY SEEDHEADS AND STUNNING PODS

❖

Clematis tangutica ◯
Papaver somniferum (annual)
Omphalodes linifolia ♀ ◯
Pulsatilla vulgaris ♀ ◯
Staphylea pinnata ◯

---

texture, they can be dried for decorative use or left to turn into winter skeletons, revealing the orange-red berries inside. A spreading, rhizomatous perennial, it will creep into empty border spaces but is rarely a pest. Divide in early spring.

Ricinus communis 'Carmencita' ♀
Castor oil plant

☼ ✳ ● **H** 1.2–1.5m/4–5ft **S** 90–150cm/3–5ft

Although a shrub in warmer countries, the true castor oil plant is usually grown as an annual in colder climates. Raise from spring-sown seed and plant out in

early summer to enjoy the exotic, lobed, bronze-red leaves. Insignificant flowers are followed by clusters of red, spiny seed capsules. All parts are poisonous.

Scabiosa stellata 'Paper Moon'

☼ ✳ ✳ ✳ **H** 45cm/18in **S** 23cm/9in

This hardy annual bears exquisite seedheads, valued for drying. The spherical flowerheads are an insipid mauve-pink with larger outer florets developing into a ball of pale, stiff, papery cells. Sow into modules or straight into the soil in spring.

KEY: ♀ *Award of Merit* ☼ *sun* ☼ *semi-shade* ● *shade* ✳ *half-hardy* ✳✳ *frost-hardy* ✳✳✳ *fully hardy* ◯ *deciduous* ● *evergreen* ◐ *semi-evergreen* **H** *height* **S** *spread*

The spring flower garden

Everyone looks eagerly for the first spring flowers, many of which flourish naturally in woodland shade. For beauties like dog's-tooth violet (Erythronium) and trilliums, it is worth creating special beds enriched with leafmould, but others can be sprinkled through beds and borders. Enjoy their dainty display before the more flamboyant flowers of summer appear.

Helleborus orientalis 'Sirius'

40

Aquilegia vulgaris
Columbine, granny's bonnet
☼ ☼ ❄ ❄ ❄ ◯ **H** 75cm /30in **S** 45cm /18in

These herbaceous perennials, easily raised from spring-sown seed, will begin flowering during their second year, in late spring. Their spurred flowers, usually in shades of pink and purple, resemble an old-fashioned bonnet. Consult seed catalogues for double forms and those with bright yellow foliage. Once established, they will seed around and, in my garden, have proved tolerant of poor, dry soil.

Dicentra 'Stuart Boothman' ♔
Bleeding heart
☼ ❄ ❄ ❄ ◯ **H/S** 30cm /12in

Delicate, blue-grey, ferny foliage appears in early spring from perennial rhizomes; good for masking the foliage of snowdrops as they die down. Two-tone pink flowers, shaped like Dutchman's trousers, provide a show from mid-spring into summer. One plant can be divided in early spring to form a carpet.

Doronicum 'Miss Mason' ♔
Leopard's bane
☼ ❄ ❄ ❄ ◯ **H/S** 45cm /18in

Give this herbaceous perennial a well-drained soil, or it has a tendency to rot away during winter. I like this variety because its 8cm (3in) wide, yellow daisy flowers are held well above the foliage from mid-spring to early summer. It combines well with leucojum and can be used as spring bedding. Divide large plants in spring or early autumn.

> **SMALL SPRING BULBS TO PLANT UNDER SHRUBS**
> ❖
>
> *Anemone blanda* (wood anemone) ♔
> *Leucojum vernum* (spring snowflake)
> *Chionodoxa forbesii* and *C.f.* 'Pink Giant' (glory-of-the-snow)
> *Erythronium dens-canis* (dog's-tooth violet) ♔
> *Puschkinia scilloides*
> *Scilla mischtschenkoana*
> *Scilla siberica* ♔

Erysimum 'Bowles' Mauve' ♔
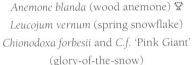
☼ ❄ ❄ ❄ ● **H/S** 75cm /30in

This evergreen, perennial wallflower earns its place in the garden by bearing its purple flowers from spring into summer. In common with most wallflowers, it appreciates well-drained, slightly alkaline soil. A trim after flowering will delay the time when an older plant needs replacing by a successor raised from cuttings struck the previous spring.

Fritillaria imperialis
Crown imperial
☼ ❄ ❄ ❄ ◯ **H** 90–120cm /3–4ft **S** 30cm /12in

Plant the large, foxy-smelling bulbs

Aquilegia vulgaris var. *stellata*

Dicentra 'Stuart Boothman'

Lunaria annua variegata

◁ **THE TALL BACKDROP**
of Fritillaria imperialis
makes a striking foil for a
clump Leucojum aestivum,
with their nodding flowers.

41

20cm (8in) deep in well-drained soil
during autumn. Early spring should
see fresh buds nosing their way up
through the soil; by late spring, they
have risen to produce a display of
bell-shaped, orange or yellow flowers,
crowned by a tuft of leafy bracts.

Helleborus orientalis
Lenten rose
☼ ❊ ✳ ✳ ✿ **H/S** 45cm/18in

These choice evergreen, herbaceous
perennials produce their saucer-shaped
flowers from late winter to mid-spring.
Promiscuous, they hybridize readily and
most plants seen in gardens are hybrids.
Flower colours can be white, cream,
green, pink and deep maroon-red,
sometimes attractively marked with
darker spots or flecks.

Leucojum aestivum 'Gravetye Giant' ♀
Snowflake
☼ ❊ ✳ ✳ ✳ ◯ **H** 60cm/2ft **S** 23cm/9in

Plant bulbs 10cm (4in) deep in autumn
in moist, well-conditioned soil to bloom
the following spring. White, nodding,
green-tipped flowers are suspended
from the main stem by slender stalks.

Lunaria annua variegata
Variegated honesty
☼ ❊ ✳ ✳ ✳ ✿ **H** 90cm/3ft **S** 60cm/2ft

Sow this biennial in the early summer of
one year to flower during the late spring
of the next. The first year's rosette of
leaves is plain green, the cream-edged
leaves being produced as the plant
rises up to produce its pink flowers.
Disc-shaped green pods turn whitish-
silver in autumn and persist all winter.

Omphalodes linifolia ♀
Venus' navelwort
☼ ✳ ✳ ✳ ✿ **H/S** 30cm/12in

Sow this pretty biennial into well-
drained soil one summer to produce
airy white flowers the following spring.
Thereafter, a rash of blue-green
seedlings will appear every autumn and
can be thinned and transplanted where
needed. So-called because the seedpods
resemble tummy buttons!

Pulmonaria saccharata
Lungwort
☼ ❊ ✳ ✳ ✳ ✿ **H** 30cm/12in **S** 45cm/18in

Among these eminently collectable
herbaceous perennials, this species is
one of my favourites. The rosette of
silver-spotted leaves persists all winter,
with stems of furry buds rising to reveal
pink flowers from early to late spring.
Remove old leaves after flowering.

Pulmonaria saccharata

KEY: ♀ *Award of Merit* ☼ *sun* ❊ *semi-shade* ✿ *shade* ✳ *half-hardy* ✳✳ *frost-hardy* ✳✳✳ *fully hardy* ◯ *deciduous* ✿ *evergreen* ✿ *semi-evergreen* **H** *height* **S** *spread*

The summer flower garden

There are so many colourful summer-flowering perennials, annuals and bulbs that creating stunning summer borders is easy. Nevertheless, planning is needed to make sure the display continues from early to late summer, when there can be a lull in the garden. Reserve a few pots of annuals like Rudbeckia 'Marmalade' to fill gaps after a midsummer overhaul.

42

Anthemis tinctoria 'E.C. Buxton'

☼ ✳ ✳ ✳ ● **H** 60–90cm /2–3ft **S** 75cm /30in

Once established, anthemis prove to be drought-tolerant border plants giving a long show of bright, daisy-like flowers. The blooms of this cultivar are palest lemon yellow with deep yellow centres. As you cut down the fading flowers, more develop; the filigree foliage persists throughout winter. May require support. Divide during autumn on sandy soils but in spring on clay.

Campanula lactiflora 'Prichard's Variety' ♔
Milky bellflower

☼ ☼ ✳ ✳ ✳ ○ **H** 1.2–1.5m /4–5ft **S** 60cm /2ft

Provide support for this tall campanula by pushing sticks into position from late spring, or planting it among the stems of dogwood. Panicles of dark, violet-blue flowers are borne in summer and early autumn. Plant in fertile, neutral to alkaline soil, keep moist and trim back after flowering for a second flush. Divide in spring or autumn.

Cleome hassleriana 'Colour Fountain'
Spider flower

☼ ✳ ✳ **H** 90–150cm /3–5ft **S** 60cm /2ft

Tall annuals like cleome and tithonia never fail to impress me. That they can produce such height and flower-power in one season from seed is truly a marvel. Allow space in the border for the hairy stems of palmate leaves, topped by elegant racemes of scented pink, white or purple flowers with long, prominent stamens. Sow under glass in spring to plant out when all danger of frost has passed. Plant in fertile soil and keep moist.

▷ **CREATE DEEP BORDERS** *to accommodate a good mix of perennials that will provide colour and shape all summer. Plug any gaps with plants such as Nicotiana sylvestris (top left) and colourful larkspurs, both raised annually from seed.*

Coreopsis verticillata 'Zagreb'
Tickseed

☼ ✳ ✳ ✳ ○

H 60–75cm /24–30in **S** 30–45cm /12–18in

An ability to tolerate poor, dry, sandy soils certainly recommends this perennial to me. Another North American daisy, it is equally happy on clay. Masses of fine, fern-like, bright green leaves are joined by a profusion of dainty, golden-yellow flowerheads in early to midsummer. The pointed petals have a simple beauty. Lift, divide and replant in spring.

Echinacea purpurea 'Magnus'
Purple coneflower

☼ ✳ ✳ ✳ ○ **H** 60–120cm /2–4ft **S** 50cm /20in

The impressive hallmarks of this North American perennial are their large pink daisies, with superb, domed orange centres opening from late summer to autumn on sturdy stems. It tolerates poor, dry soils, but the plants will be shorter. To establish several groups cheaply, raise plants from spring-sown seed. Lift, divide and replant in spring or autumn.

PLANTING HALF-HARDY ANNUALS

❖

Fill gaps in a border with colourful bedding plants like pelargoniums and *Gypsophila muralis*. Planted in early summer, they will bloom till autumn, outlasting the perennial daisies.

Inula hookeri

RELIABLE PERENNIALS FOR SUMMER

Anaphalis margaritacea ✿

Aster × frikartii 'Mönch' ♀ ✿

Campanula persicifolia ✿

Campanula 'Elizabeth' ✿

Delphinium 'Sandpiper' ♀ ✿

Dianthus 'Mrs Sinkins' ●

Dictamnus albus var. *purpureus* ♀ ✿

Helenium 'Moorheim Beauty' ✿

Hemerocallis lilioasphodelus ♀ ❂

Penstemon schoenholzeri
(syn. 'Ruby') ♀ ❂

Phlox paniculata 'Eva Cullum' ✿

Sidalcea 'William Smith' ♀ ✿

Eremurus robustus
Foxtail lily

☼ ❄ ❄ ❄ ✿ **H** 1.8–2.5m /6–8ft **S** 90cm /3ft

Buy foxtail lilies as succulent roots to plant in the autumn in well-drained but nourishing soil. Plant them with their crowns just under the surface. In late spring, a rosette of basal leaves appears, followed by the flower spike, which can be prone to late frosts. This rises to a great height and is studded with masses of pointed buds held out on thin stalks, opening to small, sugar-pink flowers with yellow pollen. The leaves die back as the flowers fade.

Inula hookeri

☼ ◐ ❄ ❄ ❄ ✿ **H** 60–75cm /24–30in **S** 60cm /2ft

Soft, hairy buds open to reveal daisy-like yellow flowers with slightly darker centres and dainty, narrow petals. Both the leaves and stems of this perennial are softly hairy. Happy plants quickly form large clumps that seem to do best in light shade and benefit from some support. Plant in moist but well-drained soil. Divide in spring or autumn.

Knautia macedonica

☼ ❄ ❄ ❄ ● **H** 60–75cm /24–30in **S** 60cm /2ft

Deep wine-red, scabious-like flowers about 2.5cm (1in) across are held on hairy, branching stems well above the basal foliage all summer. Plants are easy to raise from spring-sown seed, which enables several clumps to be grown, or you can take basal cuttings in spring. Plant in well-drained, alkaline to neutral soil.

Monarda 'Cambridge Scarlet' ♀
Bergamot, Bee balm

☼ ◐ ❄ ❄ ❄ ✿ **H** 90cm /3ft **S** 60cm /2ft

I wish I could grow these beautiful perennials, but despite their origins in dry North American scrub and woodland they dislike my poor, sandy soil. To succeed, they need moist, well-drained soil or regular watering during droughts; waterlogging is not tolerated either. In bloom, the tall stems of aromatic leaves are topped by mop-like heads of scarlet petals from midsummer to early autumn. Lift and divide the rather shallow rhizomes in spring.

Paeonia lactiflora 'Bowl of Beauty' ♀
Peony

☼ ◐ ❄ ❄ ❄ ✿ **H/S** 75–90cm /30–36in

Peonies are the prima ballerinas of the early herbaceous border, giving a short-lived but voluptuous display. When choosing, be aware that flowers can be single, semi-double, double or, as here, anemone-form. Rich pink petals surround and contrast with a central mass of creamy stamens. Plant in soil enriched with organic matter from autumn to spring, when conditions are right, shallowly planting the crown no more than 2.5cm (1in) deep.

Monarda 'Cambridge Scarlet'   *Paeonia lactiflora* 'Bowl of Beauty'

KEY: ♀ *Award of Merit* ☼ *sun* ◐ *semi-shade* ● *shade* ❄ *half-hardy* ❄ ❄ *frost-hardy* ❄ ❄ ❄ *fully hardy* ✿ *deciduous* ● *evergreen* ❂ *semi-evergreen* **H** *height* **S** *spread*

The autumn flower garden

With the onset of cooler temperatures and moist soil, the garden often takes on a new lease of life after the heat and dryness of high summer. With careful planning, a range of fresh flowers can open during late summer and continue into the autumn. Their spry beauty makes an appropriate accompaniment to fruits, seeds and autumn tints.

Kniphofia rooperi

44

Anemone × hybrida 'Honorine Jobert' ♀
Japanese anemone

☼ ☼ ❄ ❄ ❄ ◯ **H** 1.2m / 4ft **S** 75cm / 30in

Large white flowers, each with a central boss of gold stamens, open from rounded buds from late summer well into autumn. These are held on branching stems, which have risen from basal leaves during the summer. Plant during autumn in moist soil enriched with organic matter and allow plants to establish into fine clumps, as their deep, woody tap roots resent disturbance.

Aster amellus 'King George' ♀
Italian starwort

☼ ❄ ❄ ❄ ◯ **H** 60cm / 2ft **S** 45cm / 18in

Although related to Michaelmas daisies, the Italian starworts sprout out from a woody base rather than from creeping rhizomes. This makes them more fragile to grow, but they have the distinct advantage of mildew resistance. 'King George' bears large, violet-blue flowerheads with contrasting, golden-yellow centres. These perennials must have well-drained soil. Root basal cuttings in spring.

Dahlia 'Alltami Corsair' ♀

☼ ❄ ◯ **H** 1.4m / 4ft 6in **S** 75cm / 30in

The simplest approach with the tall, showy dahlias is to buy tubers and plant them 10–15cm (4–6in) deep in mid-spring. Support with canes or stakes, feed well and pinch out the growing tip at 45cm (18in) to encourage branching. This semi-cactus type bears deep crimson blooms. Feed well and they can reach 15–20cm (6–8in) across. Wait until the leaves are frosted before lifting and drying tubers. Store frost-free, covered with dryish compost. For cuttings, make tubers sprout under glass in early spring and strike the young shoots.

Gladiolus callianthus ♀

☼ ❄ ❄ ◯ **H** 75–100cm / 30–40in **S** 15cm / 6in

Plant corms 10–16cm (4–6in) deep in groups between existing plants for a lovely surprise in autumn. Long stems bearing short-lived flowers over a long period rise up above the surrounding plants. Each fragrant white bloom is delicately shaped, with beautiful dark maroon markings inside. In cold areas lift, dry and store corms in a frost-free place during winter. On my light, sandy soil they usually survive average winters.

Kniphofia rooperi
Red hot poker

☼ ☼ ❄ ❄ ❄ ◗ **H** 1.2m / 4ft **S** 90cm / 3ft

The orange-red flowers turn to yellow as they fade, making the conical flowerheads of this perennial two-tone. These are produced throughout autumn, rising on stems above the tufts of long green leaves, and certainly earn their space in the garden. Plant this South African native in soil enriched with organic matter and divide established clumps in spring.

Nerine bowdenii ♀

☼ ❄ ❄ ◯ **H** 45cm / 18in **S** 30cm / 12in

Plant bulbs into well-drained soil during spring with their necks just protruding. In exposed gardens, site along the base of a sunny wall for protection. Stems push through the soil in autumn, each bearing a beautiful, fresh pink flower. These are ideal for flower-arranging and

Aster amellus 'King George'

△ **FLOWERING FROM** *late summer to autumn,* Anemone × hybrida *is a classic of the late border.*

AUTUMN SCENE-STEALERS

Amaryllis belladonna ⊘

Aster cordifolius 'Photograph' ♀ ⊘

Cimicifuga simplex 'White Pearl' ⊘

Clematis heracleifolia 'Wyevale' ♀ ⊘

Chrysanthemum 'Mary Stoker' ⊘

Chrysanthemum 'Nantyderry Sunshine' ⊘

Helianthemum helianthoides ⊘

Helianthus salicifolius ⊘

Schizostylis coccinea 'Sunrise' ♀ ◐

some gardeners set their spare bulbs in a row in the vegetable garden for this purpose. Strappy leaves appear with the flowers. Divide after flowering.

Physostegia virginiana
Obedient plant

☼ ◐ ✳ ✳ ✳ ⊘ **H** 45–60cm /18–24in **S** 45cm /18in

Flower stems rise up in late summer and autumn, bearing tubular, pinkish-purple flowers one on top of the other, usually facing in just two directions. These are hinged and, if you push one, it will stay put, hence the common name of this perennial. They enjoy moist, fertile soil but tolerate poorer ones. Sow seed in autumn or spring; divide while dormant.

Rudbeckia fulgida var. *sullivantii* 'Goldsturm' ♀
Coneflower

☼ ◐ ✳ ✳ ✳ ⊘ **H** 60cm /2ft **S** 45cm /18in

Golden-yellow, slightly pleated outer petals contrast beautifully with the inner cone of disk florets, which are a deep chocolate-brown, glowing purple in sunlight. Of North American origin, this compact perennial will tolerate poor, dry

soils well, but grows larger and faster in fertile soils with more body. Divide rhizomatous clumps in autumn or spring.

Sedum spectabile ♀
Ice plant

☼ ✳ ✳ ✳ ⊘ **H/S** 45cm /18in

Mounds of succulent, grey-green leaves and flat heads of green buds add structure in summer. Star-shaped pink flowers, loved by bees and butterflies, open in late summer and autumn. It is worth leaving the old flowerheads on until midwinter. Ice plants make a good, solid edging to a border and thrive even

Physostegia virginiana 'Vivid'

on poor, drought-prone soils; too much fertility causes flopping. Lift, divide and replant in spring or autumn.

Tricyrtis formosana ♀
Toad lily

☼ ◐ ✳ ✳ ✳ ⊘ **H** 75cm /30in **S** 45cm /18in

This woodland plant from Taiwan makes good clumps in the dappled shade between trees, opening clusters of exotic, star-shaped white or palest pink flowers that are spotted, toad-like, with purple-red. Plant in fertile soil conditioned with leafmould. Lift, divide and replant the rhizomes in early spring.

Sedum spectabile

KEY: ♀ *Award of Merit* ☼ *sun* ◐ *semi-shade* ● *shade* ✳ *half-hardy* ✳✳ *frost-hardy* ✳✳✳ *fully hardy* ⊘ *deciduous* ● *evergreen* ◐ *semi-evergreen* **H** *height* **S** *spread*

The winter flower garden

Many of the plants featured here are bulbs that bloom in late winter. Used in conjunction with flowering shrubs, they can give the illusion of an early spring. Particularly precious are plants like Christmas rose, winter iris and pansies, capable of flowering in the depths of winter. All make welcome additions to winter posies collected for the house.

Helleborus argutifolius

Crocus tommasinianus ♖

☼ ❄❄❄ ✿ **H** 8–10cm /3–4in **S** 8cm /3in

In late winter a sunny border can be transformed into a rich carpet of pale lilac or rich purple, depending on which form of this excellent crocus is grown. Naturalizing well, they increase by seed and offsets, spreading themselves liberally through beds and lawn. All trace of the plants will have disappeared by the time serious spring and summer flowers begin their show. Plant corms 8–10cm (3–4in) deep in well-drained soil during autumn.

Cyclamen coum ♖

☼ ❄❄❄ ✿ **H/S** 5–8cm /2–3in

Delicate buds open to fresh white, pink or red flowers above new foliage in late winter. Rounded leaves vary from plain deep green through those with silvery patterning to some, like the Pewter

Group ♖, which are almost entirely silver. Plant so that tubers sit just below the surface in rich, well-drained soil. Left undisturbed, they usually self-seed.

Eranthis hyemalis ♖
Winter aconite

☼ ☽ ❄❄❄ ✿ **H/S** 5–10cm /2–4in

With leaves like bright green collars and their pretty, yellow, buttercup-like flowers, eranthis are a promise of spring in late winter. Position them so they can push through gaps in borders or to naturalize in grass. Plant tubers 5cm (2in) deep in autumn or, better still, plant when in growth. Choose good soil enriched with organic matter.

Galanthus nivalis ♖
Common snowdrop

☼ ❄❄❄ ✿ **H/S** 8–15cm /3–6in

Although there are many more exotic

snowdrops from which to choose, the charm of the common sort, with its single, nodding flowers, is hard to resist. Plant the bulbs 10cm (4in) deep in groups, ideally when in growth or when dormant during early autumn. Given rich soil that stays moist during their growth and light shade for summer, they quickly naturalize, forming attractive groups.

Helleborus argutifolius ♖
Corsican hellebore

☼ ☽ ❄❄❄ ◗ **H** 60–120cm /2–4ft **S** 90cm /3ft

A good plant for problem areas, this hellebore is tough and capable of surviving on poor, dry soils, though it would prefer a moist, humus-rich root run. Leaves composed of three spiny-toothed leaflets are deep green above and pale below. Pendent green flowers open in late winter. Remove the old flowers and leaves to make way for new ones in late spring. The seed germinates easily when ripe.

Helleborus niger 'Potter's Wheel'
Christmas rose

☼ ❄❄❄ ✿ **H** 30cm /12in **S** 45cm /18in

Rigorous selection produced this fine form of the Christmas rose, which is

Cyclamen coum

Galanthus nivalis

Iris reticulata   *Scilla mischtschenkoana*

△ **CHEERFUL WINTER ACONITES**, *one of the earliest bulbs to flower, lift the spirits in winter.*

propagated by seed commercially. Superior plants produce huge, rounded, long-lasting blooms 10cm (4in) across in late winter. Glistening white sepals with green bases surround a central cluster of golden stamens, shown off to perfection by tall stems and an outward-looking habit. Plant in good soil enriched with organic matter. Divide large clumps after flowering.

Iris reticulata ♀

☼ ❋ ❋ ❋ ◯ **H** 15cm /6in **S** 8cm /3in

Fragrant, jewel-like flowers open in late winter as the pointed leaves break through the soil. These vary in colour from pale to deep purple or blue with bright yellow markings on each outward petal. Plant groups of bulbs into well-drained soil, 8–10cm (3–4in) deep, during autumn. Apply a high-potash liquid fertilizer every two weeks while in growth and these iris will naturalize into good clumps.

Iris unguicularis ♀
Winter iris

☼ ❋ ❋ ❋ ● **H** 45–60cm /18–24in **S** 60–90cm /2–3ft

For the best show of pale lavender-blue flowers in the depths of winter, plant this iris in poor, well-drained, neutral to alkaline soil. Mine flourish in an impoverished gap between the house wall and a tarmac drive. The grass-like foliage becomes untidy, so remove dead leaves twice a year. Divide rhizomatous clumps after flowering or in autumn.

Scilla mischtschenkoana

☼ ☼ ❋ ❋ ❋ ◯ **H** 10–15cm /4–6in **S** 8cm /3in

Plant the small bulbs 8–10cm (3–4in) deep during early autumn to bloom in late winter. The pretty, pale blue flowers do not require direct light to open and therefore make good underplanting for shrubs like camellia and fothergilla. They enjoy moisture while growing, but prefer dry soil in summer.

Viola × wittrockiana
Universal Series ♀
Winter-flowering pansy

☼ ❋ ❋ ❋ ● **H** 15–23cm /6–9in **S** 23–30cm /9–12in

Brightly coloured winter pansies are hard to resist when they fill garden centres during the autumn. Their blooms open during mild midwinter spells and continue to give a grand finale in spring. Use to fill gaps in borders, as bedding displays and for containers. Plants are raised from seed sown in late spring or early summer.

WINTER FOLIAGE
◆

To provide a foliage accompaniment to these winter-flowering beauties, try *Arum italicum* subsp. *italicum* 'Marmoratum' ♀. Reaching a height of 23-60cm (9-24in), the beautifully marbled, arrow-shaped leaves appear to wither during hard frosts, then bounce back when it thaws. Produced in autumn, the foliage persists through winter and spring, then dies back in summer. Pale green cuckoo-pint type flowers appear in early summer followed by stems of bright red berries, which are poisonous.

Annuals to grow from seed

One of the easiest and cheapest ways to fill areas with colour for the summer is to sow annuals straight into the soil in spring. Once conditions are warm enough for weeds to start germinating, they can be sown. Some make excellent cut flowers, so reserve a few rows in the vegetable plot too – they will attract beneficial insects like hoverflies and bees. Fully hardy annuals can also be sown in autumn, to give earlier flowering the following year.

Convolvulus tricolor
'Royal Ensign'

48

Amaranthus caudatus
Love-lies-bleeding, Tassel flower
☼ ❄ **H** 90–150cm /3–5ft **S** 45–75cm /18–30in

These impressive plants make tassel-like panicles 45–60cm (18–24in) long of tiny, crimson-purple flowers from summer to autumn. Resembling long strands of red millet, they show up well against the large, bright green leaves. Some selections yield plants with red, green or yellow flower tassels. For the best results, keep moist and support with twiggy sticks. Collect seed in autumn.

Amaranthus caudatus

Centaurea cyanus 'Blue Diadem'
Cornflower
☼ ❄ ❄ ❄ ❄ **H** 75cm /30in **S** 15cm /6in

A classic cornfield annual, the double, deep blue flowers measure up to 7cm (2½in) across. Cornflowers cut well for vases and some seed selections cater specifically for this, with long stems and blending shades of blue, pink and white blooms. Suitable also for bedding, there are dwarf seed strains at a diminutive 20–30cm (8–12in) high.

Chrysanthemum carinatum 'Tricolor Mixed'
Painted daisy
☼ ❄ **H** 30–45cm /12–18in **S** 30cm /12in

Bred from a Moroccan native, these showy annuals bear single, daisy-like flowers up to 8cm (3in) across of white, yellow, orange or pink flowerheads banded with deeper colours. These appear above deeply divided, almost succulent, grey-green leaves. Another good strain is 'Court Jesters' ♀ with its brilliant flowers. Support with short, twiggy sticks.

Clarkia Royal Bouquet Series
Godetia
☼ ☼ ❄ ❄ ❄ ❄ **H** 60–90cm /2–3ft **S** 30cm /12in

Satiny, frilly-petalled double flowers in shades of pink, red, mauve or white are the rewards for sowing seed straight into the soil in autumn or spring. Godetias are ideal for cutting. Choose good soil of medium fertility and, even though stems are fairly sturdy, provide twiggy sticks early on.

Convolvulus tricolor 'Royal Ensign'
☼ ☼ ❄ ❄ ❄ ❄ **H** 30–40cm /12–16in **S** 30cm /12in

Growth begins upright but the stems then sprawl, making them ideal for the front of a border. Deep blue, trumpet-shaped flowers have white centres and yellow throats; up to 5cm (2in) wide, they are extremely decorative. Although related to bindweed, this annual does not have pernicious roots.

Eschscholzia Thai Silk Series
Californian poppy
☼ ❄ ❄ ❄ ❄ **H** 20–25cm /8–10in **S** 30–38cm /12–15in

Lovers of the plain and simple swear by the species *E. californica* ♀, with its shiny, bright orange petals. It is extremely fine, but so are the exotic-looking cultivars of the Thai Silk Series. Double or semi-double flowers open in a range of shimmering colours including red, pink and orange suffused with bronze. Sown into poor, well-drained soil, they will self-seed.

Eschscholzia californica

EVERLASTING FLOWERS

When dried, many hardy annuals have an everlasting quality which makes them ideal for use in flower arrangements or pot-pourri. Pick just before flowers reach maturity and hang in a cool place to dry.

Bracteantha bracteata (strawflower) Seed selections yield plants 30–90cm (1–3ft) tall, with papery flowers in bright or pastel colours.

Limonium sinuatum (statice) This perennial grown as an annual bears stiff, winged stems to 60–75cm (24–30in) bearing clusters of papery flowers in a wide range of colours.

Lonas inodora The maroon-centred, yellow flowers of this 30cm (12in) tall S. African daisy open over a long time.

Rhodanthe chlorocephala subsp. *rosea* Tall plants with papery pink, white or red bracts surrounding yellow centres.

Limnanthes douglasii

Iberis amara

49

Iberis amara 'Giant Hyacinth Flowered Mixed'
Hyacinth-flowered candytuft
☼ ❅ ❅ ❅ **H** 30cm/12in **S** 15cm/6in

Flowerheads rise into a spike of lightly scented, white, pink or red four-petalled flowers which cut well or can be used to create drifts towards the front of borders. The more petite candytuft, a favourite of children, is the shorter, flat-headed *I. umbellata*. Sow in spring or autumn.

Limnanthes douglasii ♼
Poached egg plant
☼ ❅ ❅ ❅ **H** 15cm/6in **S** 23cm/9in

Despite self-seeding with abandon, this easy plant remains within the confines of its group and, if handled with care, will not spread all over the garden. The fresh, finely divided leaves are soon studded with masses of bright, yolk-like yellow flowers, each petal edged white. Mine flower well without thinning.

Linaria maroccana 'Fairy Bouquet'
Toadflax
☼ ❅ ❅ ❅ **H** 23cm/9in **S** 15cm/6in

There are some delightful, dainty annuals among the toadflaxes. Small snapdragon blooms of jewel-like white, yellow, pink, salmon, orange, carmine or lavender, often in combination, adorn the stems of this variety while neat, linear leaves take up little space. Sown into light, well-drained soil, they self-seed freely.

Papaver commutatum ♼
Ladybird poppy
☼ ❅ ❅ ❅ **H** 45cm/18in **S** 15cm/6in

Children love to grow this easy annual because the bright red flowers, up to 8cm (3in) across, bear a black blotch at the base of each glistening petal. These rise up from low-growing rosettes of divided leaves. Poor, dry soils are tolerated well but flowers will be larger in better nourished soil and if watered.

DIRECT SOWING

To sow several different hardy annuals next to each other, first mark out generous areas using trickles of sand. Within each, draw shallow parallel drills about 15cm (6in) apart and sow thinly. Cover, firm and label. Thin the seedlings as instructed on the packet; keep moist.

Selecting clematis

There are few plants more versatile than clematis and every garden has room for at least some. In addition to being grown against walls and fences, clematis are effective either clothing trellis or, in combination with other plants, growing over an arch as well as weaving through shrubs in a border. Most clematis are easy to grow.

C. 'Vyvyan Pennell'

50

C. alpina 'Frances Rivis' ☼
Alpine clematis
☼ ☼ ❋ ❋ ❋ **H** 2.5m /8ft **S** 1.5m /5ft
Buds appear in spring, opening to reveal blue flowers followed by fluffy seedheads. Good for clothing the bases of climbing roses on a pergola, this clematis need only be pruned (after flowering) if it outgrows its space.

C. armandii
☼ ❋ ❋ ❋ **H** 5m /15ft **S** 3m /10ft
This vigorous evergreen needs a sheltered wall. Attention to siting will be rewarded by masses of vanilla-scented white flowers in early spring, set against long, shiny leaves. Plants are best left unpruned, but overgrown specimens can be cut hard after flowering.

C. 'Comtesse de Bouchaud' ☼
☼ ☼ ❋ ❋ ❋ **H** 2.4m /8ft **S** 1.8m /6ft
Large, rose-pink flowers are borne from

mid- to late summer regardless of aspect, making this a useful clematis for a north-facing wall or fence. Prune hard in late winter, but never into old wood.

C. × durandii ☼
☼ ❋ ❋ ❋ **H /S** 90cm /3ft
More of a scrambler than a climber, this indigo-flowered clematis needs a shrub for support; it is excellent for pegging down between winter-flowering heathers. Flowers are produced in midsummer and plants can be pruned back hard in autumn.

C. 'Elsa Späth' ☼
☼ ❋ ❋ ❋ **H** 2.4m /8ft **S** 1.2m /4ft
A straightforward plant for a beginner, this hybrid produces large, deep blue flowers readily all summer. Established plants need little pruning, but if growth becomes tangled, tackle this at the end of winter.

C. 'Etoile Rose'
☼ ☼ ❋ ❋ ❋ **H** 1.8m /6ft **S** 90cm /3ft
Like others in the *C. texensis* group, the deep pink flowers of this dainty plant are characteristically tulip-shaped, appearing from mid- to late summer. Prune off dead growth in late winter.

C. 'Henryi' ☼
☼ ❋ ❋ ❋ **H** 3m /10ft **S** 90cm /3ft
I love white-flowered clematis and this is one of the best. Huge blooms open during midsummer, with a show of smaller flowers in late summer and autumn. No regular pruning is needed.

C. 'Lasurstern' ☼
☼ ❋ ❋ ❋ **H** 2.4m /8ft **S** 90cm /3ft
This stalwart plant opens its massive blue flowers, each blessed with a boss of creamy anthers, during midsummer and often again in late summer. No regular pruning is needed.

C. macropetala 'Markham's Pink' ☼
☼ ☼ ❋ ❋ ❋ **H** 3m /10ft **S** 1.5m /5ft
The freely produced sugar-pink flowers have a splendid delicacy. Opening in late spring and early summer, they appear semi-double with their skirt of petal-like stamens. If pruning is necessary, carry out after flowering.

Clematis armandii

C. 'Comtesse de Bouchaud'

C. 'Lasurstern'

> ### CLEMATIS THROUGH THE SEASONS
> ❖
>
> **SPRING:**
> *C. alpina*
> *C. macropetala*
> **EARLY SUMMER:**
> *C. montana*, C. 'Nelly Moser' ♛
> C. 'Mrs Cholmondeley' ♛
> **LATE SUMMER:**
> C. 'Kardynal Wyszyński'
> C. 'Marie Boisselot' ♛
> **AUTUMN:**
> *C. flammula*
> **WINTER:**
> *C. tangutica* (seedheads)
> **LATE WINTER:**
> *C. cirrhosa* var. *balearica* ♛

△ **CLOTHING A MELLOW BRICK WALL** *are Clematis 'Snow Queen' (right) and C. 'Elsa Späth'.*

C. montana
Mountain clematis
☼ ◑ ✳ ✳ ✳ **H** 9.5m /30ft **S** 3m /10ft

This easy, rampant clematis is excellent for covering old garden buildings and scrambling into trees. White or pink blooms open in late spring. For reliable perfume, opt for named varieties like white 'Alexander' or pink 'Elizabeth'. Prune after flowering if needed.

C. 'Niobe' ♛
☼ ◑ ✳ ✳ ✳ **H** 1.8–3m /6–10ft **S** 90cm /3ft

Deep maroon-coloured mid- to late summer flowers make this a most desirable plant, which blends well with silver, purple and pink. Pruning is not vital, but stems can be cut to the topmost pair of fat buds in late winter.

C. 'Pink Fantasy'
☼ ◑ ✳ ✳ ✳ **H** 1.8m /6ft **S** 90cm /3ft

Large pink flowers open from mid- to late summer and change hue from an intense pink on opening, to pink-flushed white when mature. Said to show resistance to wilt, this clematis should be pruned hard in late winter.

C. 'Bill MacKenzie' ♛
☼ ◑ ✳ ✳ ✳ **H** 6m /20ft **S** 3m /10ft

Blooming from midsummer to autumn, silken seedheads persist well into winter. The nodding, yellow, lantern-shaped flowers are blessed with colourful red anthers. Use to scramble over pergolas and up into trees. Prune hard in late winter.

C. 'Ville de Lyon'
☼ ✳ ✳ ✳ **H** 3m /10ft **S** 1.2m /4ft

Rounded red flowers open from late summer into autumn, each graced with a central boss of golden stamens. Prune hard in late winter for the longest season of flowers.

C. 'Vyvyan Pennell' ♛
☼ ✳ ✳ ✳ **H** 2.4m /8ft **S** 90cm /3ft

One of the best doubles, the early summer blooms are an exotic mixture of violet-blue with warm flushes of carmine and yellow anthers. In common with other double-flowered clematis, pruning is unnecessary.

C. 'Niobe'

Choosing and using roses

This marvellous group of plants offers so many different attributes: there are efficient ground coverers, pretty patio roses for containers and small beds, shrubs for mixed borders and climbers to clothe vertical surfaces, not to mention bush roses for colour and cut flowers. When choosing roses, consider length of flowering time, quality of perfume and disease resistance.

R. 'Korresia'

GROUND COVER ROSES

R. Suffolk

☼ ❄ ❄ ❄ ✿ **H** 45cm /18in **S** 90cm /3ft

Some ground cover roses are large, so for smaller gardens it is useful to know this small, neat plant. Expect a show of single scarlet flowers, each decorated by golden stamens, to be produced all summer, followed by orange-red hips. Pruning is not compulsory, but I reduce mine by half in late winter.

R. 'Flower Carpet' ♛

☼ ❄ ❄ ❄ ✿

H 75cm /30in **S** 1.2m /4ft

Vigorous, disease-resistant rose introduced in 1992, with clusters of double, shocking pink flowers. 'Flower Carpet White' is easier to assimilate with other plantings.

R. 'Flower Carpet'

PATIO ROSES

R. 'Marie Pavie'

☼ ☼ ❄ ❄ ❄ ✿ **H/S** 45cm /18in

Although the idea of patio roses seems modern, this pretty dwarf polyantha type dates from 1888. Making a good, bushy shape, the clusters of fragrant white flowers, with a faint blush of pink

continue to open over a long period. A strong rose: prune out dead wood in winter.

R. 'Queen Mother' ♛

☼ ❄ ❄ ❄ ✿ **H** 40cm /16in **S** 60cm /2ft

A healthy, modern dwarf cluster-flowered rose, bred in 1991. The foliage is glossy and joined by a succession of rounded, double, pink flowers from summer to autumn. Slightly fragrant, they open fully to reveal yellow stamens. Prune in late winter by reducing the size by up to half.

R. 'Sweet Dream' ♛

☼ ❄ ❄ ❄ ✿ **H/S** 45cm /18in

What this rose lacks in perfume, it makes up for by producing masses of double, apricot-shaded flowers. Introduced 1988.

BUSH ROSES

R. 'Korresia'

☼ ❄ ❄ ❄ ✿ **H** 75m /30in **S** 60cm /2ft

I tend not to choose yellow roses, but this cheerful, cluster-flowered (floribunda) rose, bred in 1974 is one of the most popular. Light green leaves are joined by sprays of double, fragrant blooms, full of wavy petals, from summer to autumn. Prune by cutting growth back by half or more in late winter.

R. 'Margaret Merril' ♛

☼ ❄ ❄ ❄ ✿ **H** 75cm /30in **S** 60cm /24in

Since its introduction in 1978, this cluster-flowered (floribunda) rose has become popular for its deep fragrance and superbly shaped, high-centred, white blooms. Flushed faintly with pink, they contrast well with the dark green foliage and reach 10cm (4in) across. Cut back by half or so in early spring.

R. 'Mevrouw Nathalie Nypels' ♛

☼ ❄ ❄ ❄ ✿ **H** 75cm /30in **S** 60cm /2ft

This sweetly fragrant, cluster-flowered polyantha dates from 1919. Dark glossy leaves and rose-pink, semi-double flowers appear from summer to autumn.

R. 'Reconciliation'

☼ ❄ ❄ ❄ ✿ **H** 90cm /3ft **S** 60cm /2ft

I adore the peachy-blush tones of this large-flowered (hybrid tea) rose, bred in 1995. The well-formed blooms are highly fragrant and as decorative in a vase as in the garden. Prune by cutting growth to desired height in late winter.

R. 'Savoy Hotel' ♛

☼ ❄ ❄ ❄ ✿ **H** 80cm /32in **S** 60cm /2ft

This large-flowered (hybrid tea) type dates from 1989. The petals of its tall, slightly scented, double blooms are light pink on top but darker on the reverse.

SHRUB ROSES
R. 'Graham Thomas' ♀
☀ ❊ ❊ ❊ ❀ **H/S** 1.2m /4ft

The best known of David Austin's English Roses, a modern group obtained by crossing selected old roses with modern hybrid teas and floribundas to enjoy the best aspects of both. Cupped, rich yellow, double blooms emit a strong tea rose fragrance. Glorious to look at, they are slightly quartered and packed full of petals. Prune stems by half to one third in early spring. Introduced in 1983.

R. x *centifolia* 'Muscosa' ♀
Old pink moss
☀ ❊ ❊ ❊ ❀ **H/S** 1.2m /4ft

This rose (1700) produces rich pink blooms from mossy, aromatic buds.

R. 'Königin von Dänemark' ♀
☀ ❊ ❊ ❊ ❀ **H** 1.5m /5ft **S** 1.2m /4ft

This is an alba dating from 1826. Though it flowers only once in summer, it is worth growing for its fragrant, rose-pink, quartered blooms, 9cm (3½in) across.

◁ **A PERGOLA** *makes an ideal climbing frame for rambler 'Bobbie James', pruned and trained.*

R. 'Prosperity' ♀
☀ ❊ ❊ ❊ ❀ **H** 1.5m /5ft **S** 1.2m /4ft

This hybrid musk (1919) bears dark leaves and clusters of scented, double, pink-flushed, creamy-white flowers.

CLIMBING AND RAMBLING ROSES
R. 'Bobbie James' ♀
☀ ❊ ❊ ❊ ❀ **H** 10m /30ft **S** 6m /20ft

Plant with caution, as the long stems reach high into trees and up into any support offered. Large clusters of small but very fragrant creamy-white, semi-double flowers open in summer, each one lit up by central golden-yellow stamens. Introduced in 1961. Prune, if necessary, by taking out older stems in late summer.

R. 'Guinée'
☀ ❊ ❊ ❊ ❀ **H** 4.5m /15ft **S** 2.2m /7ft

Having grown this climber, I can confirm its reputation as a weak grower, as it has taken some time to settle in. But patience and good cultivation are more than amply rewarded by its deep red blooms a little over 10cm (4in) across with a perfume of exquisite intensity and quality. Introduced in 1938. Train in as many shoots as possible and cut back unwanted side shoots to short spurs in early spring.

R. 'François Juranville' ♀
☀ ❊ ❊ ❊ ❀ **H** 6m /20ft **S** 4.5m /15ft

Coral pink, slightly quilled petals have a touch of yellow at the base and open to flattish, double blooms of fruity fragrance. Choose this rambler, introduced in 1906, for pergolas and to climb up into small trees. Should pruning be necessary, cut out older stems immediately after flowering and tie in new replacement growths.

R. 'Golden Showers' ♀
☀ ❊ ❊ ❊ ❀ **H** 3m /10ft **S** 1.8m /6ft

This reliable, yellow-flowered climber dates from 1956. Large blooms are produced in succession, even on a north-facing wall.

R. 'Sympathie'
☀ ❊ ❊ ❊ ❀ **H** 3m /10ft **S** 2.5m /8ft

A vigorous climber dating from 1964, bearing clusters of cupped, double, deep red flowers from summer to autumn.

R. 'Zéphirine Drouhin' ♀
☀ ❊ ❊ ❀ **H** 3m /10ft **S** 1.8m /6ft

This extremely popular thornless climber is a bourbon, introduced in 1868. Among its attributes are deep pink, scented flowers borne over a long period. It tends to suffer from mildew, but is less prone when grown on a north-facing wall.

53

R. 'Margaret Merril'

R. 'Reconciliation'

R. 'Graham Thomas'

Ornamental grasses and bamboos

Hakonechloa macra
'Alboaurea'

Enjoying a surge of popularity, grasses are very much part of a new, relaxed style of planting. They are grown not only for their foliage but also for their decorative flowerheads, which often persist into autumn and early winter. Bamboos are chosen for their beautiful stems and oriental appearance. They rarely flower, but some species bloom simultaneously all over the country.

54

Deschampsia cespitosa 'Goldtau'
Tufted hair grass, Tussock grass
☼ ◐ ❄ ❄ ❄ 🍂

H 60–90cm /2–3ft **S** 60–75cm /24–30in
The main flowering period is from summer to autumn, when tall spikes of golden-bronze flowers emerge from tufted, rich green foliage and persist until early winter. Plant in groups for an impressive display. Keep soil slightly moist and cut down faded flowers in early spring. Divide in early spring.

Elymus hispidus
Hairy couch grass
☼ ❄ ❄ ❄ 🍃

H 45–75cm /18–30in **S** 30–45cm /12–18in
Even a single specimen of this plant is effective, its steely blue foliage at its best from spring to autumn. An occasional de-thatch will keep it pristine, but carry out a severe haircut in early spring before new growth starts. A good plant for dry, sandy soils, it is easily propagated by seed or by division in spring.

Hakonechloa macra 'Aureola' ♛
☼ ◐ ❄ ❄ ❄ ♡

H 30–38cm /12–15in **S** 30–45cm /12–18in
Set in a group of five or more, the arching mounds of this grass will amaze anyone with an eye for form and colour. Grown in a container, the flexible, bright yellow leaves, marked down their length with fine green lines, will cover its sides. *H.m.* 'Alboaurea' is similar, with green, white and yellow leaves. Pale green flowers open in panicles, late summer to mid-autumn. Divide in spring.

Milium effusum 'Aureum'
Bowles' golden grass
☼ ❄ ❄ ❄ 🍃

H 30–45cm /12–18in **S** 23–30cm /9–12in
This grass seeds itself around in partially shaded areas, creating informal drifts of bright, lime-green leaves, at their best from spring to late summer. Small, golden, flower-bearing spikes are borne in nodding panicles from late spring to midsummer. For best results, plant in rich, moist but well-drained soil. Divide in early spring.

Milium effusum 'Aureum'

Miscanthus sinensis 'Kleine Fontäne'
☼ ❄ ❄ ❄ ♡ **H** 90–120cm /3–4ft **S** 60–90cm /2–3ft
The erect, then gently arching leaves of this grass are joined by silky flower spikes in autumn. But for lasting foliage effect, choose *M.s.* 'Morning Light', whose tall green leaves have narrow creamy margins. The latter is of architectural interest all winter, with foliage turning orange-yellow. In spring, cut down to make way for new growth and divide.

Pennisetum alopecuroides 'Woodside'
Fountain grass
☼ ❄ ❄ ❄ ♡

H 60–120cm /2–4ft **S** 45–90cm /18–36in
In summer, yellow-brown flowerheads resembling bottle brushes appear on this decorative grass. These persist into autumn and associate well with the

Pleioblastus auricomus

△ ONE OF THE MOST CLASSIC *and striking of bamboos is* Phyllostachys nigra, *whose canes mature to black. Here is it seen in an extremely ornamental role, beside water.*

REVEALING THE STEMS

Bamboos like this *Phyllostachys aureosulcata* 'Spectabilis' give year-round value for little maintenance. To smarten them up, remove lower side branches and weed out weak canes, which clutter up a structured clump.

foliage as it turns golden. Grow as specimens or in groups. Plant in fertile, well-drained soil. Divide in late spring.

Phyllostachys aureosulcata 'Spectabilis'
Yellow-groove bamboo

☼ ☀ ✳ ✳ ✳ ❦

H 3–6m/10–20ft **S** 1.2–4m/4–13ft

Plenty of water and an annual spring mulch will get this beautiful bamboo off to a roaring start. The culms (canes) are custard-yellow with green grooves and the foliage is elegant and complementary. Cut out weak canes on a regular basis (*see below left*), leaving the most vigorous to mature. Remove lower side branches to expose the straight stems. Divide in early spring.

Phyllostachys nigra ♔
Black bamboo

☼ ✳ ✳ ✳ ❦ **H** 3–5m/10–15ft **S** 1.8–3m/6–10ft

Although tolerant of partial shade, the sun will show off the shiny black canes to advantage. These begin olive-green, mottled with black, and reach perfection when three years old. It makes a wonderful specimen for a large pot. Feed and water well from spring to early summer and thin out weaker shoots regularly. Divide in early spring.

Pleioblastus auricomus ♔

☼ ✳ ✳ ✳ ❦ **H** 1.2–1.5m/4–5ft **S** 90–150cm/3–5ft

This splendid bamboo will brighten up the dullest border with the light effect of its bright green and golden-yellow striped foliage. Plant away from cold, drying winds and cut down to the

CHOICE BAMBOOS AND GRASSES
❖

Arrhenatherum elatius ssp. *bulbosum* 'Variegatum' ✺

Chionochloa rubra ❦

Chusquea culeou ♔ ❦

Fargesia nitida ♔ ❦

Festuca glauca 'Elijah Blue' ❦

Festuca glauca 'Golden Toupée' ❦

Luzula nivea ❦

Melica ciliata ✺

Stipa gigantea ♔ ✿

Miscanthus sinensis 'Kleine Fontäne'

ground annually in autumn for the best results. Use in small gardens where year-round colour is required. Divide rhizomes in spring.

Stipa tenuissima

☼ ✳ ✳ ✳ ✺ **H** 45–60cm/18–24in **S** 30cm/12in

The upright, bright green leaves of this grass are topped by silver-white flowers all summer. These are borne in fluffy, feathery, waving panicles which waft readily in the breeze. Plant in drifts of three or five in light, well-drained soil and cut down to the basal clump in early winter. Split clumps in mid-spring.

55

KEY: ♔ *Award of Merit* ☼ *sun* ☀ *semi-shade* ✳ *shade* ✳ *half-hardy* ✳✳ *frost-hardy* ✳✳✳ *fully hardy* ✺ *deciduous* ❦ *evergreen* ✿ *semi-evergreen* **H** *height* **S** *spread*

Plants for summer containers

Pots, tubs, baskets and window boxes filled with plants are an ideal way of adding seasonal colour and providing focal points. Being mobile, containers can be moved around the garden as required. Although they demand regular watering and feeding, their care involves no back-breaking digging or weeding. For a summer display, plant up during late spring or early summer.

56

Argyranthemum gracile 'Chelsea Girl' ♀
Marguerite, Paris daisy

☼ ❄ ☙ **H/S** 60cm /24in

A succession of small, white, yellow-centred daisies are borne on slender stems above finely divided, fern-like foliage all summer. Use this tender perennial for a pot or as the centrepiece for a large hanging basket. Pot up in autumn and overwinter in a frost-free greenhouse. Take cuttings in summer or in spring. Be vigilant against aphids.

Begonia Illumination Series ♀

☼ ☼ ❄ ⟳ **H** 60cm /24in **S** 30cm /12in

This trailing, tuberous begonia is the ideal solution for a hanging basket hung against a shady wall. Plant out in early summer and watch its trailing stems colonize the basket, producing masses of double, brightly coloured blooms 8cm (3in) in diameter. The tubers can be dried off to store in a frost-free place during winter. Start into growth in warmth the following early spring.

Brachyscome iberidifolia
Swan river daisy

☼ ❄ ⟳ **H** 45cm /18in **S** 35cm /14in

A spreading nature makes this annual ideal for hanging baskets and window boxes. Dissected, fern-like leaves are a backdrop to masses of blue, sometimes violet or white, daisy-like flowers, each with a contrasting yellow centre, which combine well with other container plants in full sun. Sow seed under glass in spring.

Fuchsia 'Annabel' ♀

☼ ❄ ⟳ **H/S** 30–60cm /12–24in

There are many fuchsias, suiting all tastes and different containers. These tender perennials fare better out of full sun and are good for shady plantings. 'Annabel' is a bushy sort with double white blooms touched with a faint flush of pink. Take cuttings during summer and overwinter in a frost-free greenhouse. Prune plants back in early spring.

Helichrysum petiolare 'Roundabout'

☼ ❄ ☙ **H** 15cm /6in **S** 30cm /12in

Strong foliage plants are an important ingredient of successful container plantings. Felty, silvery-leaved *Helichrysum petiolare* ♀ and its cultivars are ideal to offset stronger coloured flowers. With small leaves and low, spreading growth, 'Roundabout' will not swamp a hanging basket; its grey-green leaves have cream edges. Summer cuttings will rot if kept too humid.

Argyranthemum gracile

Begonia 'Illumination Apricot'

Brachyscome iberidifolia

◁ **TRAILING**

PETUNIAS *such as Surfinia Blue Vein are hard to beat for impact with their vigorous growth and abundance of large flowers. Use them in window boxes, hanging baskets and to smother the front of large tubs.*

Verbena 'Silver Anne' ♔

☼ ❋ ❋ ♥ **H** 30cm / 12in **S** 60cm / 24in

There are several perennial verbenas with a trailing habit, ideal for containers. 'Silver Anne' is robust enough to hold its own in a basket packed with fuchsias and pelargoniums, opening scented flowerheads of pink fading to silvery pink. Take cuttings in summer and overwinter in a frost-free greenhouse. Prune ungainly plants in spring.

Mimulus × *hybridus* Magic Series
Monkey musk

☼ ☼ ❋ **H** 20cm / 8in **S** 30cm / 12in

These bushy, spreading, tender perennials hail from my favourite plant family, Scrophulariaceae, and are related to foxgloves and toadflax. Treat as annuals by sowing seed under glass in spring. The colour range is luscious, including rich reds, yellows and oranges as well as pastel shades, most with spotted throats. Ideal for shady hanging baskets and window boxes.

Pelargonium 'L'Elégante' ♔
Ivy-leaved geranium

☼ ❋ ♥ **H** 20–25cm / 8–10in **S** 20cm / 8in

The foliage of this neat, trailing, tender perennial is extremely decorative. Ivy-shaped leaves bear irregular cream edges that turn pink in good light and clusters of single white flowers are borne throughout summer. Propagate from summer cuttings and overwinter in frost-free conditions. Prune gangly, mature plants in early spring.

Pelargonium 'L'Elégante'

Petunia Surfinia Series

☼ ❋ **H** 30cm / 12in **S** 60–90cm / 2–3ft

Trailing petunias are hugely popular for window boxes and hanging baskets, as they make long stems packed full of large, trumpet-shaped flowers. Most are scented and the range includes Blue, Purple, White, Hot Pink, Blue Vein and Pink Vein. They can be propagated by cuttings but, since they are virus-prone, it is advisable to buy healthy young plants each spring.

Portulaca grandiflora Sundance Hybrids
Sun plant

☼ ❋ **H/S** 15cm / 6in

Drought tolerance is a useful asset for plants that are grown in containers. The attractive red stems and fleshy, cylindrical, needle-like foliage of this succulent South American annual blend well with aeonium, agave and pelargoniums. Sundance Hybrids have a bushy, trailing habit and bear double flowers in a range of colours that includes bright pinks, reds, orange, white and yellow. Sow seed under glass in spring.

57

PLANTING AND CARE

❖

• Make sure all containers have drainage holes; use pot feet or tiles to raise them off the ground.

• Always use good potting compost; try an equal mixture by volume of a soilless variety and John Innes No. 2.

• Do not stand pots outside until all danger of frost has past.

• At planting time, incorporate slow-release fertilizer and moisture-retaining granules into the compost.

• Apply general-purpose liquid feed at least weekly for most plants.

Winter and spring containers

Autumn is the time to remove fading summer flowers from your troughs and pots and replant them for winter and spring. Use tough evergreen shrubs and perennials to give bulk and shape, with trailing ivies and smaller pansies, bellis and primulas for colour and infill. Push dwarf-growing, spring-flowering bulbs around the roots of other plants for a seasonal surprise.

Tanacetum parthenium 'Aureum'

58

Ajuga reptans 'Braunherz' ♛
Bugle

☼ ❋ ❋ ❋ ◗ **H** 15cm /6in **S** 60cm /24in

The low rosettes of shiny, dark maroon leaves on this perennial ground cover can plug gaps in winter and spring arrangements. They even flourish in the sides of hanging baskets. Spikes of blue flowers, 15cm (6in) tall, appear in late spring and early summer. On dismantling the container, plant a bugle in the ground and it will quickly multiply, ready to supply future plantings.

Bellis perennis Pomponette Series ♛
Daisy

☼ ☼ ❋ ❋ ❋ ◗ **H/S** 10–15cm /4–6in

Sow seed in early summer to yield plants that will bloom in the autumn and spring. Neat, domed, red, pink or white double flowerheads up to 4cm (1½in) across are packed full of quilled petals. Although treated as biennials, they are perennial and the clumps can be divided after flowering. Watch out for aphids.

Brassica oleracea Osaka Series
Ornamental cabbage

☼ ❋ ❋ ❋ ◗ **H** 30cm /12in **S** 45cm /18in

Although these colourful, annual cabbages can be raised for an autumn planting from spring-sown seed, they are usually the result of impulse buying. As temperatures fall, the wavy-edged leaves towards the hearts intensify in colour to bright pink, red or creamy white. Plants remain decorative until midwinter, after which they begin to fade and to elongate.

EVERGREENS FOR WINTER AND SPRING CONTAINERS

❖

Bergenia 'Wintermärchen'

Blechnum penna-marina

Erica carnea 'Springwood White' ♛

Euonymus fortunei Emerald 'n' Gold ♛

Euonymus fortunei 'Silver Queen' ♛

Hedera helix 'Königers Auslese'

Helleborus niger ♛

Santolina chamaecyparissus ♛

Solanum capsicastrum

Thymus × citriodorus 'Aureus' ♛

Viola × wittrockiana Universal Series ♛

Carex hachijoensis 'Evergold' ♛
Golden sedge

☼ ☼ ❋ ❋ ❋ ◗ **H** 23cm /9in **S** 45cm /18in

This perennial grass has tufts of mop-like foliage that are of great decorative value to window boxes; the narrow leaves are marked along their length with an irregular, creamy-yellow stripe. Propagate by division in spring. The plants do not object to being lifted for use in the autumn and replaced in spring, as long as they are well watered.

Bellis perennis 'Prolifera'

Ornamental cabbages

Chamaecyparis lawsoniana 'Ellwood's Gold' ♈

☼ ◐ ✳ ✳ ✳ ● **H** 3m/10ft **S** 1.5m/5ft

Dense, yellow-green foliage, tipped with gold, makes this slow-growing conifer a year-round feature. Its height will be restricted by container growing. Use as a centrepiece to a large pot, or set two or more smaller specimens along the length of a window box for structure. Keep the roots moist, or the foliage will turn brown.

Gaultheria procumbens ♈
Checkerberry

☼ ◐ ✳ ✳ ✳ ● **H** 15cm/6in **S** 60–90cm/2–3ft

Attractive, aromatic, evergreen leaves are joined by little, pale pink, bell-shaped flowers in summer. By the autumn, these flowers are being followed by scarlet fruit and the leaves often turn red too, as temperatures drop. Plant this shrub in any container, using ericaceous compost as gaultherias are acid-loving. It also makes good ground cover for shade. Remove rooted suckers in spring.

Gaultheria procumbens

Ophiopogon planiscapus 'Nigrescens' ♈

☼ ◐ ✳ ✳ ✳ ● **H** 20cm/8in **S** 30cm/12in

With its shiny, almost black, strappy leaves, this hardy, evergreen perennial resembles a dark spider plant. Plant it near pale colours in order to show off its striking foliage. Ideal for hanging baskets, it is also usefully drought-tolerant. Rhizomatous roots quickly spread and send up new plants, forming a clump. Divide in spring.

Primula Wanda Series
Hybrid primrose

☼ ◐ ✳ ✳ ✳ ● **H** 10cm/4in **S** 15cm/6in

These brightly coloured primroses come in shades of yellow, blue, pink, red, burgundy, orange or white, usually with a yellow eye. In late spring, plant them into a shady corner of the garden, from where they can be lifted, divided and used again the following autumn.

Tanacetum parthenium 'Aureum'
Golden feverfew

☼ ✳ ✳ ✳ ● **H** 45cm/18in **S** 30cm/12in

Where you have used a lot of plain-green-leaved plants, find space in your container for a few young plants of this gold-leaved perennial. Its compact, basal growth consists of slightly divided, ferny, aromatic leaves that sit well in baskets and troughs. Plant out in the garden for summer and the leaves will rise up to open small, white, daisy-like flowers. Raise from seed in spring.

Vinca minor
Lesser periwinkle

☼ ◐ ✳ ✳ ✳ ●

H 10–20cm/4–8in
S 60–120cm/2–4ft

Plants of this evergreen shrub make trailing alternatives to the ubiquitous ivies. Neat, evergreen leaves are held opposite each other on long stems and are joined, mainly in spring, by pretty blue flowers. Other cultivars bear white or plum-purple blooms. There are doubles as well as plants with variegated foliage. Propagation is by division or summer cuttings.

CONTAINER GROWING TIPS
❖

- Try cultivating a stock of useful evergreens that can be lifted out of the garden in the autumn and replaced in spring.

- Check containers regularly for watering, even throughout winter. Baskets and boxes in the rain-shadow of walls are particularly susceptible to drying out.

- Hanging baskets can be vulnerable to freeze-drying for long periods when chill winds are blowing. Stand them on solid pots in a sheltered spot until milder weather returns.

- Inspect the shoots and buds of bellis, pansies and polyanthus regularly for aphids.

▽ **ALTHOUGH PRIMULAS** *can be raised from seed, these cheerful perennials are more often bought in bloom to select favourite colours.*

Unusual container plants

There is often a need for permanently planted containers, for prominent places in the garden or to embellish hard surfaces. Architectural plants make eye-catching subjects for permanent positions and some small trees, as well as many shrubs and perennials, are suitable. Restricting the roots in pots reduces their ultimate height and slows down their rate of growth. Some of these unusual plants are tender and need winter protection.

Acer palmatum var. dissectum

60

Acer palmatum var. dissectum ☼
Japanese maple
☼ ☀ ❄ ❄ ❄ ◐ **H** 1.8m /6ft **S** 3m /10ft
Japanese maples make elegant trees for permanent containers; my own mature maple has been growing happily in the same wooden half-barrel for the last ten years. The bright green, young spring foliage matures into finely dissected, lobed leaves that turn orange and red in autumn, and tiny, purple-red flowers mature into glistening, winged fruits. Even the winter tracery of its domed, spreading branches is appealing. Shelter from winds and late frosts.

Agapanthus campanulatus
African blue lily
☼ ❄ ❄ ❄ ◐
H 60–120cm /2–4ft **S** 45cm /18in
Although these showy, rather variable perennials are hardy, containerizing means they can be moved to a sheltered position for the winter. Rounded flower heads, 10–20cm (4–8in) across, are borne on tall stems rising above strap-shaped leaves. These heads are usually composed of

bright blue flowers, though they can be pale or darker blue or even white. Apply liquid fertilizer every two to three weeks from spring to flowering in summer.

Cordyline australis 'Torbay Dazzler'
Cabbage palm
☼ ❄ ❄ ◑ **H** 2.5–3m /8–10ft **S** 90–250cm /3–8ft
Extraordinarily showy plants, cabbage palms provide an architectural feast with their eruption of long, spiky leaves. Those of 'Torbay Dazzler' are striped and margined with creamy yellow, with pink flushes towards the base. Move under the protection of glass or to a sheltered spot for the winter, as their leaves are prone to damage from cold winds.

Agapanthus campanulatus

Corylus avellana
'Contorta' ☼
Corkscrew hazel,
Twisted nut
☼ ☀ ❄ ❄ ❄ ◐
H/S 4.5m /15ft
For an unusual winter feature, choose this shrub whose stems twist and spiral as they grow. The leaves drop in autumn to reveal sculptural stems, further decorated by the usual 5cm- (2in-) long

pale yellow hazel catkins in late winter. Underplant with early-flowering bulbs and marble-leaved arums. Remove suckers and any unwanted stems during the winter.

Melianthus major ☼
Honey bush
☼ ❄ ❄ ◐ **H** 1.2–1.8m /4–6ft **S** 90–180cm /3–6ft
Valued for its silvery blue-green, tooth-edged leaflets, this tall, imposing shrub behaves more like a herbaceous perennial if left outside during cold winters. In anything but a sheltered position, it would die off, but plants in pots can be brought under glass for winter. Grow melianthus as a lone specimen or as a bold ingredient for a large mixed container planting.

Polystichum polyblepharum
Japanese tassel fern
☼ ❄ ❄ ❄ ◐ **H** 60–75cm /24–30in **S** 90cm /3ft
I love this hardy fern and enjoy the promise held in its upright coils of new fronds in spring. At first, they are covered in golden hairs, which persist around the margins of older fronds like sparse eyelashes. For the best results, move into a greenhouse for the winter. The spores are freely produced and often germinate in the pots of other plants.

Rhododendron yakushimanum
'Heinje's Select'

◁ **THE LARGE, BLUE-GREEN** *leaflets of the honey bush* (Melianthus major) *make a striking silhouette.*

Prunus incisa 'Kojo-no-mai'
Fuji cherry

☼ ❋ ❋ ❋ ◯ **H/S** 2.5m /8ft

A small tree with much sculptural beauty, this diminutive, ornamental cherry excels as a potted specimen and, as such, grows slowly, remaining in the same pot for many years. Enjoy its tracery of branches in winter, its mass of delicate, single, pale pink spring blossoms opening from red buds and the foliage, which turns red in autumn.

Rhododendron yakushimanum

☼ ❋ ❋ ❋ ● **H/S** 90–180cm /3–6ft

Olive-green leaves are coated with silvery hairs when young and felted beneath with the softest pale brown. Water and feed regularly in summer to ensure a good set of buds, which show pink in spring, opening to white flower clusters. Plant in ericaceous compost and use a liquid feed balanced for acid-lovers.

Sciadopitys verticillata ♈
Japanese umbrella pine

☼ ☼ ❋ ❋ ❋ ●

H 10–20m /30–70ft **S** 6–8m /20–25ft

Umbrella pines are impressive specimen plants, especially when young, with whorls of glossy, linear leaves like the spokes of an umbrella. Mine has reached a neat, conical shape 2.7m (9ft) high and 90cm (3ft) wide in 11 years and is still growing in a large Versailles tub. Keep moist; give a well-balanced liquid feed fortnightly from spring to midsummer.

Vaccinium corymbosum ♈
Highbush blueberry

☼ ☼ ❋ ❋ ❋ ◯ **H/S** 1.5m /5ft

Few gardeners will have a sufficiently acid soil to grow blueberries well, but anyone can plant them into ericaceous compost in a container. The shrub's arching shoots bear oval leaves and pale,

bell-shaped flowers in late spring, followed by decorative, edible berries. The foliage turns red in autumn. For the best fruit, choose two different cultivars, such as 'Bluecrop' and 'Herbert'.

PERMANENT CONTAINER PLANTS
❖

Buxus sempervirens ♈ ●
Eucomis bicolor ◯
Hakonechloa macra 'Alboaurea' ◯
Hosta sieboldiana var. *elegans* ♈ ◯
Mirabilis jalapa ◯
Phormium 'Sundowner' ♈ ●
Phyllostachys nigra ♈ ●
Pinus sylvestris 'Beuvronensis' ♈ ●
Pleioblastus auricomus ♈ ●

GROWING TIPS FOR PERMANENT SUBJECTS
❖

- Unless otherwise stated, use a mixture of equal parts John Innes No. 2 potting compost and a soilless potting mix for containers.

- Do not plant small specimens straight into large containers, as their roots will be surrounded by too much wet compost and may rot. Start them off in small pots and pot them on gradually, when necessary, in spring.

- A spring application of an appropriate slow-release fertilizer will ensure healthy growth. Some subjects will also benefit from a dose of well-balanced liquid fertilizer every two to four weeks from spring to midsummer.

- If the soil at the top of the container becomes eroded, topdress with a layer of fresh compost.

KEY: ♈ *Award of Merit* ☼ *sun* ☼ *semi-shade* ● *shade* ❋ *half-hardy* ❋ ❋ *frost-hardy* ❋ ❋ ❋ *fully hardy* ◯ *deciduous* ● *evergreen* ● *semi-evergreen* **H** *height* **S** *spread*

Plants for pools

Aquatic plants not only add to the beauty of a pond, they are also essential for its well-being. Submerged, oxygenating plants revitalize the water and the floating leaves of sun-lovers like water lilies shade part of the surface and discourage the rapid build-up of algae. The roots of aquatic plants are also great for removing minerals on which the algae feed.

62

Aponogeton distachyos
Water hawthorn

☼ ◐ ❋ ❋ 🍃 **S** 1.2m / 4ft

The long, oval, floating leaves of water hawthorn make a change from the rounded pads of lilies. White, fragrant, hawthorn-like flowers with purple-brown anthers open in spring and autumn and are held just above the water on forked branches. Divide the rhizomes of mature plants when dormant and repot into aquatic baskets. Roots must be 30–90cm (1–3ft) deep.

Ceratophyllum demersum
Hornwort

☼ ◐ ● ❋ ❋ ❋ ⟳ **S** indefinite

The slender stems of this useful oxygenator are clothed with whorls

Aponogeton distachyos

▷ **PYGMY WATER LILIES** *like Nymphaea 'Pygmaea Helvola' are ideal where space is restricted, or to build up a collection in a moderately sized pond.*

of fine, forked leaves, giving an overall feathery appearance. Few roots are produced, though the stems sometimes root into the mud at the bottom of the pond. Stem tips form into resting buds and sink for winter, drifting back up in spring. Propagate simply by pulling away some stem and floating it in water. Grows in water 60–90cm (2–3ft) deep.

Eichhornia crassipes
Water hyacinth

☼ ❋ 🍃 **H/S** 45cm / 18in

It is hard to think that such an exotic aquatic has become a weed of tropical waterways worldwide. The inflated leaf stalks allow the water hyacinth to float, while dark, purplish roots hang down into the water. In hot summers, stalks of pale blue flowers marked with yellow and purple are produced. Lift and overwinter on trays of moist, soilless compost at a minimum temperature of 13°C (55°F).

Hottonia palustris
Water violet

☼ ❋ ❋ ❋ ⟳ **H** 30–90cm / 1–3ft **S** indefinite

As the water warms up in early spring, growth rises to the pond surface. Long stems bear deeply divided foliage above and below water. Stems of pale pinkish-lilac flowers are borne in spring. Plant in the muddy bottom of still, preferably slightly acid, shallow water, to 45cm (18in) deep. Propagate by stem cuttings in spring and summer.

Hydrocharis morsus-ranae
Frogbit

☼ ❋ ❋ ❋ ⟳ **S** indefinite

Running stems produce new plantlets, so frogbit soon spreads to cover an area of water with its floating leaves like tiny, kidney-shaped lily pads. Small, papery, white flowers with yellow centres appear in summer. The plants are mostly free-floating, but will root into shallow mud, sinking to overwinter as buds. To propagate, cut plantlets away from the parents. Needs a water depth up to 30cm (12in).

Myriophyllum aquaticum
Parrot's feather, Diamond milfoil
☼ ✳ ✳ ✿ **H** 30cm /12in above water **S** indefinite

Submerged or marginal, parrot's feather pokes its stems of feathery foliage above water and will climb happily up the pond's banks. Submerged leaves are longer than emergent ones; the summer flowers are so tiny that nobody really notices them. Propagate by cuttings. Grow in baskets of loamy soil in water 15–90cm (6–36in) deep.

Nymphaea 'Froebelii'
Water lily
☼ ✳ ✳ ✳ ✿ **S** 90cm /3ft

Although ideal for smaller ponds, including barrel ponds, the 10–13cm (4–5in) diameter flowers are still a good size. These are deep pinkish-red with central stamens of orange-red. Its leaves are an attractive bronze as they unfurl in spring. Plant in a water depth of 15–30cm (6–12in). Propagate by division of rhizomes in spring. Separate offsets or remove plantlets.

Nymphaea 'Pygmaea Helvola' ♀
Pygmy water lily
☼ ✳ ✳ ✿ **S** 25–40cm /10–16in

For restricted areas, or moderate ponds where more than one lily is to be grown, this is ideal. Leaves, heavily mottled with purple, are attractive and not overpowering. They are joined by semi-double, clear yellow flowers

Eichhornia crassipes

Nymphaea 'Froebelii'

63

USING AQUATIC BASKETS
❖

Containers for aquatics are usually made of plastic and resemble baskets with wide mesh sides. Line first with hessian, before setting the plants in good loam. Do not use fertilized compost, as this will enrich the water and encourage algae. Finish off with a good layer of pebbles to settle the loam before carefully lowering into the pond. Containers can be raised to the correct planting depth by standing on a ledge or blocks. Fertilizers specially formulated for use in ponds can be bought in sachet or tablet form for hungry feeders like water lilies.

5–8cm (2–3in) across in summer. Plant in depths of 15–23cm (6–9in). Propagate by lifting, dividing and replanting into baskets for aquatics.

Nymphoides peltata
Fringed water lily
☼ ✳ ✳ ✳ ✿ **S** indefinite

Suitable for a wildlife pool, the leaves resemble small lily pads and grow from long runners, quickly colonizing the water surface. Bright yellow flowers 2cm (¾in) with fringed petals are held above the water by stout stalks in summer. Water depth 15–60cm (6–24in). Propagate by division in spring or separate runners in summer.

Stratiotes aloides
Water soldier
☼ ✳ ✳ ✳ ✪ **H** 15cm /6in above water **S** indefinite

A curious free-floating plant, the rosette of spiky leaves hangs half in and half out of the water. As the temperature drops in autumn, rosettes sink to the warmer depths of the pond, rising again the following spring. White flowers are sometimes borne in summer. New plants form from spreading stems and can be separated in spring. Water depth 30–90cm (1–3ft).

Marginals and bog garden plants

Marginals are plants that like to grow in the shallow water at the edges of ponds and streams. They are an important group for pond wildlife. Bog garden plants prefer to grow in moist soil, but do not usually like standing in water for any length of time; in fact they usually dislike waterlogging and need surprisingly good drainage.

Butomus umbellatus

64

Butomus umbellatus ♈
Flowering rush
☼ ❊ ❊ ❊ ♡ **H** 90–150cm /3–5ft **S** 45cm /18in

Tall, rush-like foliage is joined by showy umbels, 10cm (4in) across, of fragrant, dark-centred, pink flowers in late summer. The water depth can vary between 5–25cm (2–10in), with plants either flourishing in the mud at the edges of wildlife pools, or growing from baskets standing in deeper water. Divide rhizomes in early spring, just before growth starts.

Caltha palustris ♈
Marsh marigold, Kingcup
☼ ❊ ❊ ❊ ♡ **H/S** 45cm /18in

One of the easiest and most satisfying marginals to grow, marsh marigolds are relatively well behaved and, although they spread into good clumps, are not invasive. Toothed, kidney-shaped leaves make a deep green background for bright yellow, waxy flowers borne in spring. Plant in boggy ground, or very shallow water to 15cm (6in) deep. Divide in early spring or late summer.

Iris pseudacorus 'Variegata'
Yellow flag
☼ ❊ ❊ ❊ ♡ **H** 90–150cm /3–5ft **S** 90cm /3ft

The young spears of this iris, rising sword-like and half green, half creamy-yellow, make an exciting contrast with other foliage in spring. They are joined by yellow flowers in mid- to late summer. An extremely vigorous iris, this is only suitable for medium to large-sized ponds and needs supervision. Lift, divide and replant immediately after flowering.

Menyanthes trifoliata
Bogbean
☼ ❊ ❊ ❊ ♡ **H** 20–30cm /8–12in **S** indefinite

With dark pinkish-maroon spreading rhizomes and trifoliate leaves that stick upwards from the water surface, bogbean is a handsome plant even before its stems of small summer flowers appear. These open white from pink buds and each of the five petal lobes is fringed. Water depth should be 15–23cm (6–9in). Cut rhizomes into sections and peg into wet earth.

Caltha palustris 'Flore Pleno'

Myosotis scorpioides

CREATING A BOG GARDEN
❖

- Unless the soil is naturally moist, create a bog garden by laying an inexpensive or old flexible pond-liner over a flat-bottomed hole about 60cm (2ft) deep.

- Pierce the liner here and there across the bottom with a garden fork to allow drainage.

- Shovel in a 5cm (2in) layer of pea shingle over the liner to keep the drainage holes clear.

- The most efficient way to water is below soil level, so place a seep hose, or an old hosepipe perforated with holes, onto the shingle with the inside end sealed and the other end clear of the hole.

- Fill the hole with good soil enriched with organic matter; tread to firm.

- Bog gardens can be made adjacent to a pond by extending the same liner, but this can be unwise, as the bog garden may draw water from the pond, causing the level to drop.

- To conserve moisture, apply a 5cm (2in) mulch of well-rotted compost, composted bark, mushroom compost (though not where acid-loving plants will grow) or pebbles while the soil is damp.

- Water an existing bog garden using a seep hose at the surface.

◁ **IRIS PSEUDACORUS 'VARIEGATA'**
*establishes easily and quickly in a pond.
The foliage provides bright colour and
strong vertical shapes.*

Although individuals spread
into large colonies, they can be
controlled. Divide in early spring
or autumn.

Primula pulverulenta ♀
Candelabra primula

☼ ❋ ❋ ❋ ◑

H 60–90cm / 2–3ft **S** 30cm / 12in

This striking primula overwinters
as a small rosette, which grows
and sends up stout flower stems
covered by white, mealy 'farina'
in late spring. Deep pink flowers
with darker eyes are arranged in several
whorls up the stem. Plant into wet,
boggy neutral to acid soil, enriched with
organic matter. Sow seed as soon as it is
ripe, or divide the plant while dormant.

Schoenoplectus lacustris subsp. tabernaemontani 'Zebrinus'
Striped rush

☼ ❋ ❋ ❋ ◆

H 90cm / 3ft **S** 60cm / 2ft

Virtually leafless, grey-
green stems are patterned
as if by a strobe light, with
creamy-white bands.
Sometimes the stems revert
to green and these must be
cut out before they take
over. This versatile rush can
be planted in boggy
poolside soil or submerged
by up to 30cm (12in) of
water. Propagate by rooting
sections of rhizome in
spring or summer.

Myosotis scorpioides
Water forget-me-not

☼ ◑ ❋ ❋ ❋ ◑ **H** 15–30cm / 6–12in **S** 30cm / 12in

This makes a really good waterside plant,
with branching, rhizomatous stems
growing first outwards, then upwards.
Familiar, pale-eyed, blue flowers are
borne in early summer. Grow in wet soil
or plant into an aquatic basket stood in
shallow water, with the surface no deeper
than 10cm (4in). Propagate by sowing
seed on to wet compost, or planting
ready-rooted sections of rhizome.

Osmunda regalis ♀
Royal fern

☼ ❋ ❋ ❋ ◑ **H** 1.2–1.8m / 4–6ft **S** 1.2–3.7m / 4–12ft

The stately fronds are fresh green,
unfurling themselves in spring from
massive rhizomes. Spores are produced
on fertile fronds, which bear clusters of
rust-brown sporangia towards their tips.
In autumn its colour turns orange and
russet. Plant in moist, preferably acid
soil, enriched with organic matter.

Scrophularia auriculata 'Variegata'
Water figwort

☼ ❋ ❋ ❋ ◑ **H/S** 90cm / 3ft

In spring there is a ground covering of
attractive foliage, the leaves having
creamy, irregular margins and markings.
Having enjoyed this display, watch the
rosettes of leaves elongate into tall stems
bearing typical figwort flowers of
greenish-maroon throughout summer.
Plant into wet, boggy soil for the best
results. Divide clumps or root basal
cuttings in spring.

65

Trollius × cultorum 'Lemon Queen'
Globeflower

☼ ◑ ❋ ❋ ❋ ◑ **H** 60cm / 2ft **S** 45cm / 18in

I have always loved globeflowers and
in particular these hybrids, with their
characteristic bowl-shaped flowers.
In this case they are pale, shimmering
lemon, but can be yellow, orange
or gold; they appear from spring to
midsummer. Plant into moist soil
enriched with organic matter. Lift,
divide and replant as growth begins
or after flowering.

Primula pulverulenta   *Osmunda regalis*

Plants for damp, shady sites

Never view damp, shady areas of the garden as a problem, because they give an opportunity for growing a wide range of plants that would never thrive in thin, parched soils in full sun. Shade can be turned into a positive asset and in fully lit gardens often has to be specially created for the comfort of people and plants alike.

Aruncus dioicus �
Goatsbeard

☼ ☼ ❊ ❊ ❊ ♡ **H** 1.2–1.8m /4–6ft **S** 1.2m /4ft

For goatsbeard to reach its full potential it needs moisture at the roots; this will enable it to tolerate full sun or shade. Tiny cream flowers are packed into feathery panicles in early and midsummer. The fern-like foliage is susceptible to attack by slugs and snails. This is a good perennial for a relaxed, wild-looking area. Divide in autumn or in early spring.

SHADY CHARACTERS
❖

TREES AND SHRUBS
Hydrangea macrophylla cvs ♡
Leycesteria formosa ♡
Prunus padus ♡

UNDERPLANTINGS
Asplenium scolopendrium ♥ ◆
Astilbe 'Straussenfeder' ♥ ♡
Athyrium filix-femina ♥ ♡
Blechnum spicant ♥ ◆
Cimicifuga racemosa ♥ ♡
Dryopteris filix-mas ♥ ♡
Filipendula rubra 'Venusta' ♥ ♡
Hosta 'Wide Brim' ♥ ♡
Impatiens walleriana cvs
Polygonatum odoratum ♡
Uvularia grandiflora ♥ ♡

Blechnum penna-marina

☼ ☼ ❊ ❊ ❊ ◆ **H** 15–20cm /6–8in **S** indefinite

This fern is a useful evergreen to plant between taller specimens in a dark, damp corner of the garden where the soil has been enriched with leafmould. Here, the rhizomes will spread and form a mat, sending up divided fronds that start bronze-tinted and turn deep green. It is also good for shady winter containers. Divide at any time.

Camellia × williamsii 'Donation' ♥

☼ ❊ ❊ ❊ ◆ **H** 2.2–4.5m /7–15ft **S** 1.5–2.5m /5–8ft

One asset of this popular camellia is that once the large, pink, semi-double flowers are finished, they shatter quickly, the petals falling in a pink pool beneath the plant. Plant into well-conditioned, moist but well-drained, slightly acid soil. Make sure it remains moist in summer, when flower buds are setting. Cuttings, taken in late summer, are a challenge to root.

Camellia × williamsii 'Donation'

Darmera peltata ♥

☼ ☼ ❊ ❊ ❊ ♡

H 90cm–180cm /3–6ft **S** 90cm /3ft

A good performer, this perennial thrives along the banks of streams and in the moist soil of a bog garden. The umbrella-like leaves grow tall and lush, turning from green to red in autumn. Stout stems bearing heads of small pink flowers appear in late spring. Divide in autumn or early spring.

Epipactis gigantea
Giant helleborine

☼ ☼ ❊ ❊ ❊ ♡

H 30–40cm /12–16in **S** 60–150cm /2–5ft

To my mind, this North American native is among the easiest of hardy orchids. Plant in a cool, shady place where the soil can be enriched by leafmould and stays moist but does not get waterlogged. Spreading by rhizomes, a wide colony soon forms. Greenish-yellow flowers marked with maroon appear in late spring and early summer. Divide in early spring.

Hydrangea quercifolia ♥
Oak-leaved hydrangea

☼ ☼ ❊ ❊ ❊ ♡ **H** 1.8m /6ft **S** 2.5m /8ft

As the botanical name suggests, this shrub bears large leaves shaped like those of an oak tree. Conical panicles of white flowers open from midsummer to autumn, becoming pink-tinged with age.

△ IN MOIST SOIL *beneath trees, candelabra primula, hosta and ligularia thrive along stream margins.*

67

At this point they contrast with the foliage as it turns bronze-purple before falling. Plant in moist soil enriched with organic matter. Pruning is generally unnecessary.

Kirengeshoma palmata ♀

☀ ❋ ❋ ❋ ♡ **H** 60–120cm / 2–4ft **S** 75cm / 30in

Stems of slightly lobed, bright green leaves end in delicate showers of nodding, bell-like, pale yellow flowers. Plant in moist, slightly alkaline soil enriched by leafmould and it will spread by rhizomes. This perennial from Japan looks great in a shaded woodland garden. Divide in autumn or as growth begins in spring.

Hydrangea quercifolia

Matteuccia struthiopteris ♀
Ostrich fern, Shuttlecock fern

☀ ❋ ❋ ❋ ♡ **H** 1.2m / 4ft **S** 90cm / 3ft

Spring is the best time to appreciate the beauty of the shuttlecock fern, when the erect new 'shuttlecock' fronds burst out from each crown, maturing to fine structures with opposite ranks of narrow pinnae (frondlets). Shorter, spore-bearing fronds with inrolled margins appear in late summer and autumn. The creeping rhizomes produce separate ferns a sensible distance from the parent. Propagate either by lifting these or by sowing spores when ripe.

Smilacina racemosa

Smilacina racemosa ♀
False Solomon's seal

☀ ☀ ❋ ❋ ❋ ♡ **H** 75–90cm / 30–36in **S** 60cm / 2ft

Candles of small, creamy-white flowers are produced during mid- to late spring at the tips of stems bearing attractive foliage. Use as bold clumps in moist, rich soil around shrubs as well as in conjunction with spring bulbs. They also combine beautifully with hostas, astilbes and ferns. Divide this rhizomatous perennial in autumn or early spring.

Trillium cuneatum
Wake robin

☀ ☀ ❋ ❋ ❋ ♡ **H** 30–60cm / 1–2ft **S** 30cm / 12in

Ever since I first saw a large clump of this stunning North American perennial, I coveted this plant for my garden. Patience is required, as growth from tiny rhizomes is slow. Each reddish stem holds a collar of three large, mottled leaves, from the centre of which a deep maroon flower with upright petals opens in spring. Plant in moist soil enriched with organic matter. Propagate by dividing clumps after flowering.

Plants for dry shade

Most gardens have a patch of dry shade, perhaps under a tree or alongside a hedge. These impoverished areas are usually inhospitable, all the goodness and moisture being sucked out of the soil by greedy tree roots. Plants that can tolerate dry shade are invaluable but you should always condition your soil by digging in plenty of organic matter and add a mulch after planting.

Symphoricarpos x doorenbosii 'Mother of Pearl'

Aucuba japonica 'Rozannie'
Spotted laurel, Japanese laurel

☼ ☼ ☼ ❄ ❄ ❄ ❖ **H/S** 90cm /3ft

Despite the common name, this aucuba is not spotted but bears glossy, mid-green, slightly toothed leaves. It is bisexual and the spring show of small maroon flowers should set a reliable crop of red fruit; the assistance of hand pollination may be required. Root semi-ripe cuttings in summer.

Cyclamen hederifolium ♔

☼ ❄ ❄ ❄ ❄ ♡ **H** 10–13cm /4–5in **S** 15cm /6in

Jewel-like flowers in shades of pink with darker bases unfurl from pointed buds in late summer and autumn, preceding the beautifully patterned leaves. The flower stalks coil, bringing the developing seedpods to ground level. Leave the surrounding soil undisturbed and these plants will self-seed. Plant under trees, in soil enriched with organic matter, where the ground will be dry during summer dormancy. Choose young potted plants rather than dried tubers.

Epimedium x versicolor 'Sulphureum' ♔
Barrenwort, Bishop's mitre

☼ ❄ ❄ ❄ ❖ **H** 30cm /12in **S** 90cm /3ft

Grown chiefly for their pointed, heart-shaped foliage, the epimediums are closely related to shrubby berberis, in whose family they belong. They are all lovely, making first-class ground cover with impenetrable root systems. This one bears coppery-tinged spring foliage and yellow flowers in spring. Clip back the old leaves in late winter, before the new growth appears. Divide in autumn.

Euphorbia amygdaloides var robbiae ♔
Mrs Robb's bonnet

☼ ☼ ☼ ❄ ❄ ❄ ❖

H 30–60cm /1–2ft **S** 30cm /12in

An unassuming perennial, this euphorbia knits into a good, ground-covering colony able to thrive in poor, dry soils. Plants are brightened, from spring to summer, by greenish-yellow flower structures that peep like eyes from above glossy foliage. Its sap is an irritant however. Spreads by rhizomes and portions can easily be separated to make new plants.

Geranium phaeum
Dusky cranesbill, Mourning widow

☼ ☼ ☼ ❄ ❄ ❄ ♡ **H** 75cm /30in **S** 45cm /18in

A tall cranesbill grown for its small but unusual deep maroon flowers, which complement the maroon, marked, lobed leaves. Flowers can also be violet-blue, pale mauve or white and are borne in late spring and early summer. Suitable for planting under shrubs and trees, it brings an element of lush coolness to dry areas. Divide in autumn.

Liriope muscari ♔
Lilyturf

☼ ☼ ❄ ❄ ❄ ❖ **H** 30cm /12in **S** 45cm /18in

Clump-forming, tuberous perennials produce tufts of long leaves, joined in autumn by spikes of bobbly purple flowers. Most effective grown as a group, lilyturf associates well with autumn crocus and colchicum. Pick over periodically to remove brown leaves. For a lighter effect, track down *L.m.* 'Gold Banded' with gold-, then cream-edged leaves. Lift, divide and replant in spring.

Epimedium x versicolor 'Sulphureum'

Polystichum setiferum

68

△ **WOOD SPURGE** (Euphorbia amygdaloides) *flourishes and spreads in the dry shade beneath trees in a woodland setting. Acid, yellow-green flower structures combine well with blue scillas.*

GROUND COVER FOR DRY SHADE
❖

Bergenia 'Bressingham Ruby' ●

Danae racemosa ♈ ●

Daphne laureola ●

Euonymus fortunei

Emerald 'n' Gold ♈ ●

Geranium macrorrhizum 'Album' ♈ ⬭

Lunaria annua 🍃

Lamium maculatum 'Pink Pewter' ●

Mahonia aquifolium 'Apollo' ♈ ●

Meconopsis cambrica ♁

Omphalodes cappadocica ♈ ●

Pachysandra terminalis ♈ ●

Phlomis russeliana ♈ 🍃

Skimmia japonica subsp. *reevesiana* ●

Vancouveria hexandra ♁

Viburnum davidii ♈ ●

69

Luzula nivea
Snowy woodrush

☼ ☀ ❋ ❋ ❋ ● H 30–60cm / 1–2ft S 45cm / 18in

In my garden I chose this perennial to grow under the canopy of a Judas tree and the plants have thrived. Easily raised from autumn- or spring-sown seed, each makes a tuft of leaves edged with fine white hairs. In summer, stems bearing clusters of pure white flowers appear. Clumps can be divided in spring.

Osmanthus heterophyllus 'Purpureus'

☼ ☀ ❋ ❋ ❋ ● H/S 1.8–2.5m / 6–8ft

These holly-like, slow-growing evergreen shrubs are useful for small gardens. Although they tolerate dry shade, be warned that in poor soil their growth will be extremely slow. Nevertheless, this purple-leaved form is attractive when, in spring, the new growths are a shiny blackish-purple, later turning dark green. Propagate by summer cuttings.

Polystichum setiferum ♈
Soft shield fern

☼ ☀ ❋ ❋ ❋ ● H/S 90cm / 3ft

Although ferns are associated with damp, shady places, the soft shield fern can cope with dry conditions. Its new fronds look like octopus tentacles and mature to soft, much divided, mossy green pinnae. Older fronds bear plantlets that can be detached and inserted into small pots of compost. Or lay an entire frond plus plantlets on the surface of moist compost. Divide multi-crowned clumps in spring.

Symphoricarpos × doorenbosii 'Mother of Pearl'
Snowberry

☼ ☀ ❋ ❋ ❋ ♁ H/S 1.8m / 6ft

Because of its indestructible nature, the snowberry is often dismissed as a garden plant, but it is a good gap-filler for shady corners. Thickets of arching stems with neat, rounded leaves produce small, bell-shaped, greenish-white flowers in summer, followed by large crops of white fruit. Because of their suckering habit, propagation is easy. Dig out unwanted plants to control their spread.

DIVIDING A FERN
❖

To split this large, soft shield fern I lift the whole plant, then drive two forks back to back between two crowns of growth, finally teasing the roots apart by hand.

KEY: ♈ *Award of Merit* ☼ *sun* ☀ *semi-shade* ● *shade* ❋ *half-hardy* ❋ ❋ *frost-hardy* ❋ ❋ ❋ *fully hardy* ♁ *deciduous* ● *evergreen* ⬭ *semi-evergreen* **H** *height* **S** *spread*

Plants for dry, sunny sites

There is a wealth of plants which enjoy dry, sunny conditions and are naturally drought-tolerant. Many have hairy or silvery foliage and their leaves tend to be small and narrow, to prevent excessive moisture loss. In general, these plants dislike having wet feet in winter and a well-drained soil is essential for their survival.

Rosmarinus officinalis 'Majorca Pink'

70

Aster turbinellus ♈
☼ ❋ ❋ ❋ ❋ ○ **H** 1.2m/4ft **S** 60cm/2ft

Wiry stems bearing small, narrow leaves will need support, but are happy to lean against nearby shrubs. From early to late autumn, masses of pale violet flowers with yellow centres open, resembling small Michaelmas daisies. Tolerant of poor soils, this perennial from the USA comes back year after year. Lift, divide and replant in spring or autumn.

Catananche caerulea 'Bicolor'
Cupid's dart
☼ ❋ ❋ ❋ ❋ ○ **H** 60–75cm/24–30in **S** 30cm/12in

Easily raised from spring-sown seed, catananche will bloom in its first summer and can be dotted in groups throughout a border. This short-lived perennial is slender, producing tufts of long, narrow grey-green leaves and, from midsummer to autumn, solitary, papery flowerheads, each perched on a long slender stalk. The flowers of the species are blue, but in this variety they are white with purple centres.

Aster turbinellus

Cercis siliquastrum ♈
Judas tree
☼ ☼ ❋ ❋ ❋ ❋ ○ **H/S** 2.5–10m/8–30ft

Sun and good drainage are the prerequisites of this Mediterranean tree, which can grow on a single main stem or, multi-stemmed, as a shrub. The pink flowers are pea-like and the kidney-shaped leaves glaucous blue-green. Plant out when young, then avoid disturbance. Choose a sheltered spot because the flower buds (arising directly from both old and young branches) and young leaves are vulnerable to late spring frosts. Propagate by autumn-sown seed.

Geranium palmatum ♈
☼ ☼ ❋ ❋ ❋ ◗ **H** 60–90cm/2–3ft **S** 90cm/3ft

This stately geranium has proved hardy in my garden. Although perennial, treat as a biennial. It can be sown, or will seed itself freely to germinate in spring and build up rosettes of large, intricately lobed leaves, providing valuable winter foliage. Branching stems of generous purple-pink flowers with deeper centres appear the following summer.

Linaria triornithophora
Three-birds-flying toadflax
☼ ❋ ❋ ❋ ◗ **H** 90cm/3ft **S** 60cm/2ft

A perennial which flowers all summer long and spreads itself about, weaving its thin stems between other plants, should be more widespread, yet the three-birds toadflax is relatively uncommon. The whorled flowers resemble pale pink-purple snapdragons, each having a long spur, purple-striped throats and yellow on the lower lip. They are easily propagated by seed or division.

Lotus hirsutus
Hairy Canary clover
☼ ❋ ❋ ❋ ◗ **H/S** 75cm/30in

Given good drainage, this small, silvery Mediterranean shrub is easy to grow and will seed itself into undisturbed soil. Expect pink-tinged stems clothed with small, softly hairy grey-green pinnate leaves. Pea-like white flowers flushed with pink are borne in summer, followed by purplish seedpods. Stems may die back in winter, so prune to tidy up in early spring. Take cuttings in summer.

PLANTS FOR A SHINGLE GARDEN
❖

Allium sphaerocephalon ○
Helichrysum italicum ◗
Iris chrysographes ○
Penstemon 'Pink Dragon' ◗
Phygelius × rectus 'Moonraker' ◗
Pinus sylvestris 'Beuvronensis' ♈ ◗
Rosmarinus officinalis 'Majorca Pink' ◗
Sedum 'Herbstfreude' ♈ ○
Teucrium fruticans 'Azureum' ♈ ◗

△ **COMBAT DROUGHT** *with a shingle-mulched bed. Moisture is conserved and weeds suppressed so that cypress, yucca, helianthemum and gazanias can thrive in the well-drained soil.*

OREGANO HAIRCUT

❖

Not only does *Origanum laevigatum* 'Herrenhausen' flower for a long period, attracting butterflies and bees, but if you cut it back after blooming it will make a mat of evergreen foliage for the winter.

Olearia 'Waikariensis'
Daisy bush

☼ ✳ ✳ ✳ ● **H/S** 1.8m /6ft

With shared origins in New Zealand, this shrub is similar to the more common *O. × haastii*, but bears longer leaves. Olive-green leaves are silvery-white beneath and stems are pale too. White daisy-like flowers are produced from early to midsummer, followed by many seeds with hairy parasols. Plant in well-drained soil. Take semi-ripe cuttings in late summer.

Origanum laevigatum
'Herrenhausen' ♀
Oregano

☼ ✳ ✳ ✳ ● **H** 60cm /2ft **S** 45cm /18in

Neat, aromatic leaves, a plentiful summer-long display of small, closely packed purple-pink flowers and a neat basal rosette of evergreen foliage are valuable attributes. This sun-lover also attracts many butterflies and bees. Provide support if stems are not to sprawl and prune down to the basal rosette after flowering. Plant in well-drained soil. Propagate by division.

Salvia sclarea var. turkestanica
Clary sage, Sweaty Betty

☼ ✳ ✳ ✳ ●

H 75–120cm /30–48in **S** 60–90cm /2–3ft

This biennial or short-lived perennial has a strong scent which, though pleasant at first, lingers like stale sweat. Basal growth of large leaves builds up during the first year, then persists throughout winter. In summer, spikes of white and purple flowers with persistent, papery bracts rise up. Raise from spring-sown seed; the plants will self-seed thereafter.

Salvia sclarea var. turkestanica

Verbena bonariensis

☼ ✳ ✳ ✿ **H** 1.5m–1.8/5–6ft **S** 60cm /2ft

Strong stems bearing long, narrow, toothed dark green leaves rise narrowly, making this a useful perennial for slotting in between other plants. Heads packed full of dark buds persist at the ends of branches, opening to small purple flowers from summer into autumn. Plant in well-drained soil. Sow seed in spring.

Verbena bonariensis

KEY: ♀ *Award of Merit* ☼ *sun* ✴ *semi-shade* ✿ *shade* ✳ *half-hardy* ✳✳ *frost-hardy* ✳✳✳ *fully hardy* ✿ *deciduous* ● *evergreen* ✿ *semi-evergreen* **H** *height* **S** *spread*

Exposed and windy sites

The key to success when growing plants in an exposed site is to create a windbreak to protect vulnerable species from cold, drying winds. Once this is established, ordinary plants should thrive on the calm side of the barrier. A mixture of tough trees and shrubs will filter the wind more effectively than solid barriers, which can create currents and draughts.

Chamaecyparis nootkatensis 'Pendula' ♛
Nootka cypress

☼ ❄ ❄ ❄ ● **H** 15m/50ft **S** 6m/20ft

Use tall, tough conifers among the ingredients of an informal windbreak some distance from the house. The Nootka cypress has interesting bark that sheds in plates. The branches of this pendulous cultivar sweep in an elegant, horizontal fashion, bearing sprays of sharp but scale-like, strong-smelling foliage joined by greenish cones.

Crataegus monogyna 'Stricta'
Hawthorn

☼ ☼ ❄ ❄ ❄ ○

H 6–9m/20–30ft **S** 3–3.7m/10–12ft

All hawthorns can tolerate exposure to cold and wind, but this narrow, columnar form with erect branches

72

is probably the toughest of all. It will suit a wild, countryside garden and bears masses of fragrant white blossom in late spring, followed by red fruits much-loved by birds. Propagation by budding or grafting is usually left to the nursery.

Laburnum × watereri 'Vossii' ♛
Golden rain

☼ ❄ ❄ ❄ ○ **H/S** 7.5m/25ft

The biggest deterrent to planting these useful small trees is that all parts of the plants are highly poisonous if eaten. With good reason, the parents of young children worry about the temptation of seedpods when they fall. This cultivar produces a reduced crop of seed and bears exceptionally long racemes of yellow, pea-like flowers, up to 60cm (2ft) in length, from late spring.

TOUGH CHOICES FOR EXPOSED PLACES

❖

Cotinus coggygria ♛ ○ (smoke bush)
Cornus alba 'Spaethii' ♛ ○ (dogwood)
Fagus sylvatica ♛ ○ (beech)
Mahonia aquifolium ●
Quercus robur ♛ ○ (common oak)
Salix caprea ○ (willow)
Sorbus aucuparia ○ (rowan)
Taxus baccata ♛ ● (yew)

Philadelphus 'Beauclerk' ♛
Mock orange

☼ ☼ ❄ ❄ ❄ ○ **H/S** 2.5m/8ft

One of the tall philadelphus would make a good, floriferous addition to an informal windbreak. This cultivar is grown for its profusion of highly scented, single white flowers, 5cm (2in) across, borne in late spring and early summer. Prune by thinning out older stems immediately after flowering. Propagate by summer cuttings, or hardwood cuttings in winter.

Populus × candicans 'Aurora'
Balm of Gilead

☼ ❄ ❄ ❄ ○ **H** 15m/50ft **S** 6m/20ft

The ultimate size of this tree may sound offputting, but young specimens can be cut down or 'stooled' every year in late winter, so that plants grow as multi-stemmed shrubs to about 2.5–3m (8–10ft) high. This results in even larger heart-shaped leaves marked with white, cream and pink. Keep poplars well away from buildings, as their roots can be invasive.

Prunus spinosa
Blackthorn, Sloe

☼ ❄ ❄ ❄ ○ **H** 5m/15ft **S** 3.5m/12ft

The common blackthorn is a pretty, small tree or large shrub, often appearing from seed in a garden. Early

Philadelphus 'Beauclerk'

◁ **THE COYOTE WILLOW** *from North America* (Salix exigua) *makes a thicket of elegant dark stems, clothed in contrasting, silvery foliage. This tough willow thrives best on moist, sandy soils.*

73

Spiraea x *vanhouttei*

Viburnum opulus 'Xanthocarpum'

to blossom in spring, the tiny white flowers shine out against the dark wood. They are followed by round black fruit, or sloes, which are sour, but good for making sloe gin. Prune to thin and shape trees or shrubs during winter.

Salix exigua
Coyote willow
☼ ❋ ❋ ❋ ○ **H** 3.7m/12ft **S** 5m/15ft

One of the loveliest of willows, this species shows at its best when the wind sways the thickets of dark stems and whispers through their long, narrow, silvery foliage. Yellow catkins appear in spring at the same time as young, silky leaves. Thrives in moist, sandy soils but can tolerate some dryness. Propagate by hardwood cuttings in winter.

Sorbus aria 'Lutescens' ♀
Whitebeam
☼ ◐ ❋ ❋ ❋ ○ **H** 10m/30ft **S** 8m/25ft

Choose this whitebeam to add a delightful small tree to a boundary windbreak. Generously sized, tooth-edged leaves are silvery above and below, though their surfaces turn grey-green with age. This gives the tree a shimmering effect, augmented in spring by bunches of white flowers, which turn into dark red berries. Thrives on chalky or acid soil.

Spiraea x vanhouttei ♀
☼ ❋ ❋ ❋ ○ **H** 2m/6ft **S** 1.5m/5ft

Most of the spiraeas make good infills to plug holes in a windbreak. This one is a superb sight in early summer when the arching stems are smothered with clusters of small white flowers, so the

whole shrub resembles a cascading white waterfall. Prune established spiraea bushes after flowering by thinning out the older stems. Propagate by summer cuttings.

Viburnum opulus 'Xanthocarpum' ♀
Guelder rose
☼ ◐ ❋ ❋ ❋ ○

H 3–3.7m/10–12ft **S** 2.5–3m/8–10ft

The yellow-fruited guelder rose makes an attractive addition to a natural looking windbreak. Maple-like leaves are joined, in late spring and early summer, by heads bearing small, central fertile flowers, surrounded lacecap-style by sterile florets. These turn to showy bunches of yellow fruit then, as a finale, the leaves turn red before falling. It tolerates chalk. Propagate by semi-ripe cuttings taken in summer.

Plants for acid soils

Gardeners who find themselves gardening on acid, or lime-free, soil will be able to grow plants largely forbidden to those whose soil is alkaline or even neutral. Most acid-loving plants appreciate coolness and moisture, so light shade and a soil enriched with organic matter are an advantage. The best known acid-lovers are heathers and rhododendrons, which I have omitted in favour of more unusual plants.

Meconopsis grandis

74

Andromeda polifolia
Bog rosemary
☼ ☼ ❄ ❄ ❄ ❧ **H** 40cm/16in **S** 60cm/2ft

A low-growing shrub native to peat bogs, andromeda is best grown towards the front of a raised bed, or in a rock garden to avoid soil splashes and being swamped by other plants. Its needle-like foliage is reminiscent of rosemary and pink, bell-shaped flowers appear from spring to early summer. Mulch to retain moisture. Propagate by summer cuttings or layering.

Cassiope lycopodioides ♈
☼ ☼ ❄ ❄ ❄ ❧ **H** 8cm/3in **S** 25cm/10in

Plant in a similar situation to andromeda, so that its mat-like growth can be appreciated on a bank or raised area. Scale-like leaves strung tightly around long stems lend a mossy appearance, belied by the white, bell-shaped flowers

in late spring. Plant in a position sheltered from late frosts. Propagate by summer cuttings or layering.

Celmisia spectabilis subsp. magnifica
☼ ☼ ❄ ❄ ❄ ❧ **H/S** 30cm/12in

The splendid New Zealand celmisias prefer a cool, moist climate but it is possible to grow them in hotter, drier areas as long as the soil is enriched with organic matter and never waterlogged. Perennial rosettes of long silvery leaves are joined by sturdy stems bearing large, white, daisy-like blooms with yellow centres, mainly during early summer. Divide rosettes in spring.

Enkianthus campanulatus ♈
☼ ☼ ❄ ❄ ❄ ❧ **H** 2.5–3m/8–10ft

Being able to provide this shrub with cool, moist roots is as important as acid soil. Then it will thrive, making clusters of leaves under which hang a prolific display of delicate looking, bell-shaped flowers in spring and early summer. Pink-veined over cream, they have a shell-like appearance. Take cuttings in summer.

CREATING AN ACID BED
❖

It is possible to grow acid-loving plants even in gardens with unsuitable soils and sites, if a special bed is created.

Choose a lightly shaded site, perhaps against a north-facing wall, and make a raised bed, about three bricks deep. Excavate to a depth of 30cm (12in) on neutral soils; on chalky soils, take out more and line the base with a sheet of polythene, with holes pierced for drainage. Put lime-free stones or rubble in the base to improve drainage and refill with neutral topsoil containing plenty of added leafmould, pine-needle mould and well-rotted garden compost. Leave to settle and add more organic matter before planting.

Gaultheria mucronata ♈
☼ ☼ ❄ ❄ ❄ ❧ **H/S** 90–120cm/3–4ft

These compact, bushy shrubs look somewhat surreal when covered in the round white, pink or purple-red berries for which they are grown. These follow small, white or pink-flushed, urn-shaped early summer flowers. Male and female varieties are needed to set fruit, usually with one male to a group of females. The glossy foliage is also pleasant. Propagate by summer cuttings.

Enkianthus campanulatus

Gaultheria mucronata 'Stag River'

◁ **THE GIANT DAISY HEADS** *of* Celmisia spectabilis *are long-lasting and attract attention. A raised bed can be enriched with leafmould to create a moist, slightly acidic root run.*

closest to the Himalayan habitat of this perennial. In these conditions, plants will grow tall and healthy but in a hot, dry climate they are usually stunted and short-lived. Huge rosettes of hairy leaves build up and stunning blue flowers with orange anthers open in early summer. Raise from fresh seed.

Gentiana sino-ornata ♀
☼ ❋ ❋ ❋ 🜨 **H** 5–7cm/2–3in **S** 15–30cm/6–12in

Cultivate gentians in large carpets and they will provide a superb sight in full bloom. This one bears linear, grass-like foliage, against which the blue flowers glisten in autumn. Unless the garden conditions are naturally cool and moist, site in light shade and ensure that the soil is moist and enriched with organic matter. Propagate by division or by rooting offsets in spring.

Grevillea rosmarinifolia ♀
☼ ❋ ❋ ● **H/S** 2.2m/7ft

Choose a sheltered position for this drought-tolerant, exotic-looking Australian shrub and it will prove hardy on well-drained soils. Mine begins flowering in early spring, continuing well into summer. New buds then start to set. The flowers are pinkish-red, with curved styles that protrude like antennae. Site away from paths as the needle-like foliage is prickly. Take summer cuttings. Thin to reduce size after flowering.

Kalmia latifolia ♀
Calico bush
☼ ❋ ❋ ❋ ● **H/S** /1.8–3m/6–10ft

Consistent with most other acid-lovers, this shrub prefers a cool, moist

environment if it is to grow healthily to its full height. From late spring to summer, the flower buds look like piped sugar icing and open to clusters of bowl-shaped pink flowers patterned by paler stamens and dark pollen. This is a good woodland plant that resents being container-grown. Propagate by summer cuttings or layering.

Meconopsis grandis ♀
Himalayan blue poppy
☼ ❋ ❋ ❋ 🜨 **H** 60–120cm/2–4ft **S** 60cm/2ft

A cool, moist environment where the soil is rich yet well-drained comes

Kalmia latifolia **'Clementine Churchill'**

Pieris 'Forest Flame' ♀
☼ ☼ ❋ ❋ ❋ ● **H** 2.2–3.5m/7–12ft **S** 1.8m/6ft

The brilliant red new growths of this shrub are vulnerable to spring frosts, so site with care. The leaves turn to pink, cream and finally green as they mature. The white flowers are arranged in drooping panicles in mid- and late spring. Plant pieris in well-drained soil nourished by plenty of organic matter and sheltered from wind. Summer cuttings are a challenge to strike.

ACID-LOVING SHRUBS
❖

Camellia japonica 'Doctor Tinsley' ♀ ◗
Crinodendron hookerianum ♀ ◗
Corylopsis pauciflora 🜨
Cornus florida 🜨 (dogwood)
Disanthus cercidifolius ♀ 🜨
Embothrium coccineum ●
Fothergilla major ♀ 🜨
Hamamelis vernalis 'Sandra' 🜨
Illicium anisatum ●
Rhododendron 'Sappho' ♀ ◗
Styrax wilsonii 🜨
Vaccinium corymbosum ♀ ◗

KEY: ♀ *Award of Merit* ☼ *sun* ☼ *semi-shade* ● *shade* ❋ *half-hardy* ❋ ❋ *frost-hardy* ❋ ❋ ❋ *fully hardy* 🜨 *deciduous* ● *evergreen* ◗ *semi-evergreen* **H** *height* **S** *spread*

Plants for chalky soil

Chalk is often seen as a disadvantage, but there are many wonderful plants that flourish even on thin soils over chalk. Add plenty of organic matter to chalky soils in order to help plants establish quickly as well as to conserve moisture. For a gardener new to chalky soil it is vital to check the tolerance of each plant before buying or trying to grow it.

Cistus × purpureus

76

Clematis 'Huldine'

☼ ☀ ✳ ✳ ✳ ✳ ○ **H** 3–4.5m /10–15ft **S** 1.8m /6ft

Like the rest of the clematis tribe, 'Huldine' thrives on chalk. Small but plentiful white flowers with mauve reverses are borne in summer. Plant deeply in autumn and feed plants well during late spring and early summer. Prune to within short spurs of older wood in late winter.

Cistus × purpureus ♈
Rock rose

☼ ✳ ✳ ✳ ◗ **H/S** 90cm /3ft

On well-drained soil, cistus should prove to be hardy, if short-lived, shrubs. Their sticky shoots are aromatic in the sunshine and studded with deep pink, tissue-like flowers throughout summer. Each petal is marked at the base with a dark maroon

spot. Propagate by summer cuttings. Untidy shrubs can be pruned in early spring, but do not cut into old wood.

Cornus mas ♈
Cornelian cherry

☼ ☀ ✳ ✳ ✳ ✳ ○ **H/S** 4.5m /15ft

Grown as a large shrub or small tree, the cornelian cherry varies in height according to the depth and fertility of soil. The leaves, 10cm (4in) long, turn red and purple in autumn before falling. The branches light up in late winter when clusters of small, fragrant yellow flowers open. These are followed by red, edible fruit in summer. Propagate by seed or summer cuttings.

Erysimum cheiri 'Blood Red'
Wallflowers

☼ ✳ ✳ ✳ ◗ **H/S** 45cm /18in

Wallflowers are short-lived perennials treated as biennials. Sow directly into soil in late spring, plant out in autumn and enjoy their richly scented flowers the following spring. Alternatively, buy

Cornus mas

△ **SITED INSIDE** *the protective canopy of other trees here,* Magnolia × loebneri *'Leonard Messel' looks magnificent when wreathed with its starry blooms in spring.*

CHALK-TOLERANT SELECTION

Buddleja davidii 'White Profusion' ♀ ♡

Cytisus × *kewensis* ♀ ●

Dianthus cvs

Eremurus stenophyllus ♡

Euonymus alatus ♀ ♡

Fuchsia 'Genii' ♀ ♡

Helianthemum 'Fire Dragon' ♀ ●

Hibiscus syriacus 'Oiseau Bleu' ♀ ♡

Lilium candidum ♀ ♡

Syringa vulgaris 'Madame Lemoine' ♀ ♡

Paeonia mlokosewitschii

Papaver orientale 'Beauty of Livermere'

bare-rooted plants in autumn. This cultivar bears deep red blooms and blends well with pansies, tulips and daffodils in beds or containers.

Hypericum 'Rowallane' ♀
St. John's wort

☼ ☽ ✳ ✳ ✳ ❂ **H** 1.8m /6ft **S** 90cm /3ft

Choose a sheltered site for this shrub, which will reward your consideration by producing a fine display of bright golden-yellow flowers, 5–8cm (2–3in) across, from late summer to autumn. These are cup-shaped and decorated by prominent stamens. Thin out older stems in spring. Propagate by summer cuttings.

Magnolia × *loebneri* 'Leonard Messel' ♀

☼ ☽ ✳ ✳ ✳ ♡ **H** 8m /25ft **S** 6m /20ft

One look at the starry, pale lilac-pink flowers of this magnolia in spring reveals that there is *M. stellata* in its parentage. Plant in moist soil for this small tree or large, rounded shrub to achieve its potential. Pruning is not a good idea with magnolias, so take its eventual size into account when siting.

Paeonia mlokosewitschii ♀
Caucasian peony

☼ ☽ ✳ ✳ ✳ ♡ **H/S** 90cm /3ft

This elegant, herbaceous perennial sends up stems of attractively divided, blue-green foliage and its distinctive, bowl-shaped, soft yellow flowers open in late spring and early summer. As with all peonies, make sure the crowns are buried by no more than 2.5cm (1in), or they may not flower well. Propagate by division in autumn, taking care not to damage the roots.

Papaver orientale 'Beauty of Livermere' ♀
Oriental poppy

☼ ✳ ✳ ✳ ♡ **H** 90–120cm /3–4ft **S** 90cm /3ft

The many cultivars of these early-summer flowering herbaceous perennials are drought-tolerant and suitable for chalky soils. This bears blooms 10–15cm (4–6in) across, composed of huge, silky-red petals with a black blotch at the base of each. Provide with some twiggy support. Propagate by division in spring or autumn, or root cuttings in late autumn.

Romneya coulteri ♀
Tree poppy

☼ ✳ ✳ ♡ **H/S** 1–1.8m /3–6ft

Romneyas are perennials that either thrive and colonize or quietly die. One is advised to plant in the shelter of warm, sunny walls in well-drained soil, yet there are apocryphal stories of colonies invading buildings and pushing through the floors. Stems of glaucous, grey-green leaves bear white summer blooms with golden stamens. Propagate by 8–10cm (3–4in) root cuttings in spring.

Scabiosa caucasica 'Clive Greaves' ♀
Scabious, Pincushion flower

☼ ✳ ✳ ✳ ❂ **H/S** 60cm /2ft

Attractive to bees and butterflies as well as making excellent cut flowers, the large lavender-coloured blooms are most desirable. Borne in mid- and late summer, the flowerheads are 8cm (3in) across with pale centres. Young plants can be difficult to establish, so make sure they are not overgrown by neighbouring plants in the border. Divide established plants or take basal cuttings in spring.

KEY: ♀ *Award of Merit* ☼ *sun* ☽ *semi-shade* ● *shade* ✳ *half-hardy* ✳✳ *frost-hardy* ✳✳✳ *fully hardy* ♡ *deciduous* ● *evergreen* ❂ *semi-evergreen* **H** *height* **S** *spread*

80

ACKNOWLEDGMENTS

The producers and authors would like to thank the following for their support in the creation of this book: **Mrs P Mitchell**, **Mrs R Hills** and **Victoria Sanders** for allowing us to photograph in their gardens; **Paul Elding** and **Stuart Watson** at BOURNE VALLEY NURSERIES, Addlestone, Surrey for their advice, materials and studio; and **John Swithinbank** for all the support and encouragement he gave to Anne.

PICTURE CREDITS

KEY: t = top; b = bottom; l = left; r = right; c = centre; D = designer; G = garden

A-Z BOTANICAL COLLECTION: **Anthony Cooper** 26bl; **Terence Exley** 54bl; **Jiri Loun** 54t; **Adrian Thomas Photography** 62t.

Neil Campbell-Sharp: 10bl; G: Tintinhull 26br; G: Westwind 28tr, 31t, G: Applecourt, Hants 35bl; G: Pictons 44b; G: Barrington Court, Somerset 45t; 45br, G: Marwood Hill 55tl; G: Bosvigo 58bl; G: Westwind 59l, G: Homecourt 66b, G: Tintinhul 67br.

Andrew Lawson: 6bl, 7t, 36t, 53t, 57bl, 58t, 58br, 65t, 67t, 68bl.

Jacqui Hurst: 41tl.

PHOTOS HORTICULTURAL PICTURE LIBRARY: 6t, 11, 27l, 29tr, 30b, 37bc, 48br, 53bl, 54br, 55r, 56 all, 57t, 59r, 60b.

DEREK ST ROMAINE PHOTOGRAPHY: 51t.

THE GARDEN PICTURE LIBRARY: **David Askham** 32b; **Chris Burrows** 44tr, 49tl; **Brian Carter** 9b, 10br, 12b, 15br, 31br, 34br, 37br, 73bl, 77r; **Densey Clyne** 52b; **Kathy Charlton** 15bc; **Jack Elliot** 26bc; **Ron Evans** 13bl, 18r, 19b. **Christopher Fairweather**: 13br, 15t, 38bc, 63tl, 71bl; **John Glover** 8b, 10bc, 17bl, 17bc, 18bl, 21b, 23bl, 24br, 28l, 31bl, 33br, 34bl, 33t, 40t, 44br, 46bl, 46t, 47r, 49tr, 53br, 62bl, 67br, 68t, 68br, 70bl, 73br, 74t, 75b, 76br; **Sunniva Harte** 50bc; **Marijke Heuff** 38br, 50br; **Neil Holmes** 14 all; 17br, 19tl, 20t, 23b, 32tl, 45bl, 64br; **Jacqui Hurst** 31bc, 38bl; **Roger Hyan** 48bl; **Lamontagne** 51b, 61l, 73tl, 85t; **Jane Legate** 28b; **Mayer/Le Scanff** 6bc, 8t, 33bl, 36bl, 71br; **Sidney Moulds** 43br; **Clive Nichols** 9t, 21t, 64bl, 65bl, 74br; **Marie O'Hara** 39l; **Jerry Pavia** 41tr, 43bl, 76bl; **Laslo Puskas** 53bc; **Howard Rice** 26t, 34bc, 36bc, 36bl, 37bl, 40bl, 47c, 50t, 50br, 62r, 63tr, 64tl, 69t, 77l; **David Russel** 65br; **Stephen Robson** 24tr; **Gary Rogers** 33t; **JS Sira** 15bl, 17t, 23br, 25br, 44br, 41b, 43tr, 46br, 47l, 50bl, 74bl; **Friedrich Strauss** 61r; **Brigitte Thomas** 22tr; **Juliette Wade** 76tl; **Mel Watson** 37 all, 72; **Steven Wooster** 25bl, 42tr.

Steve Gorton 6br, 7b, 12t, 13t, 16r, 18tl, 19tr, 22tl, 30t, 36t, 39r, 48t, 49bl, 49br, 55bl, 57br, 60t, 63b, 69b, 70t, 71tr.

Peter Anderson 16l, 20b, 24bl, 24bc, 27r, 29bl, 29br, 32r, 35br, 71tl.